ISBN 10: 151430662X

ISBN 13: 9781514306628

Cover art by Maureen St. Clair

Editing, layout, and interior illustrations
by Rachel Morgan & Lucy Morgan

Inquiries regarding requests to reprint all or part of this book
should be addressed to BK Halifax Meditation Centre at
halifax@ca.brahmakumaris.org

To the Ocean of Virtues

What is Virtue?

Virtue is the beauty of a person. It is what makes them lovely and unusual. It is the color, form, and shape of their personality. It is the way they do things; the way they move, speak and dress. They may have no money, but if a person has virtues, they will always seem rich, for everything that is close to them will be filled with quality.

Virtue shines outwards into everything: into the body, into the environment and ultimately into the fibre of the planet itself. It fills what is empty, heals what is sick, and settles what is troubled.

But underneath virtue must be silence, for silence is the gold that sets off the jewels and protects them from scattering. In silence a person can see how the wealth is to be spent, where to invest it and make its value grow.

There is a story that tells of an earth that was once peopled by men and women who knew instinctively how best to be with each other. And the story goes that the first of these was a woman and she was called Lakshmi, which means Goddess of Wealth or Virtue, and the second was a man – Narayan, the one who became perfect through the silence of yoga.

When silence and virtue characterise the relationship between two people, there is harmony. When silence and virtue live together in one person, there is perfection. Perfection is a possibility or there would be no word for it.

Anthea Church, Inner Beauty

Introduction to the Alphabet Series: Virtues A-Z

This series of sessions was offered at the Brahma Kumaris meditation centre in Halifax, Nova Scotia every Monday night over a period of 26 weeks. Our intention was to give people a practical experience of the virtues of the soul. Usually, virtues are considered the domain of morality. However, it is our understanding that they are instead descriptions of the quality of energy of the soul, expressed through the body in actions. We noticed that many people who come to meditate do not have a vocabulary of virtues. Therefore, this book is an experiment with building a virtues literacy.

To begin...
Once upon a time there were two facilitators who loved to design learning experiences for themselves and others. They loved thinking of a group, focusing on a theme or topic, and developing a learning activity that would take an abstract idea, like a virtue, and turn it into a practical, transformative experience for souls. Sometimes it worked well, and at other times it was less effective. But they always loved the creative process of dreaming up a new way of thinking, feeling and doing things.

The 26 virtues emerged as they went along. Some of the early ones were chosen and designed together as a start-up, while some - because of scheduling - were designed and facilitated by one person accompanied by God. As a co-facilitator, he's divine! Ego never gets in the way and there is a wealth of knowledge available to the facilitator and then to the group.

In this series, the facilitator does very little talking or teaching. This allows for discovery, exploration and some sharing amongst the learners (the facilitator is a learner also). There are some handouts and props, but many of the activities require very little beyond time and willing souls.

Here is the list of virtues that emerged as we worked through the 26 weeks:

A – accuracy	M – maturity
B – benevolence	N – newness
C – cooperation	O – optimistic
D – discipline	P – peace
E – enthusiasm	Q – quick
F – fearlessness	R – responsibility
G – gentleness	S – sweet
H – humility	T – tirelessness
I – introversion	U – understanding
J – joy	V – victory
K – knowledge	W – wisdom
L – liberation	X-Y-Z – (e)xpanding your zeal!

Special thanks to so many resources that inspired the sessions – Dadi Janki, Anthea Church, Mike George & Carmen Warrington.

In designing these sessions and this guide we had a great time in soul conscious creativity. We wish you a similar experience. Have fun and be creative – remember that each design can be modified and used for other virtues. We are always looking to bring newness. Enjoy exploring the inner world of virtues for expression in the outer world.

Feel free to send your new ideas via email to the Halifax Brahma Kumaris Centre.

All the best,

Debbie and Judy

INTRODUCTORY SESSION

Setting Intention - To introduce virtues and the energy of the soul

Meditation – suggestion to include commentary *Today I Will Meditate on a Virtue* by Carmen Warrington on cd *Today I Will 20-30 minutes*

Experiencing the Virtue -
a. Welcome the group to the first session of the Alphabet Series – Exploring Virtues.

b. Let them know that this series is about spiritual literacy: – an alphabet of virtues. Each week we will approach one virtue per session for 26 sessions. Let them know that they can drop in as they can make it and enjoy each session on its own. In each session we will summarize the virtue of that session for ourselves and keep it, developing our own dictionary of virtues. Ask for ideas: examples of A virtues, B virtues?

c. Ask: What do they think a virtue is anyway? Hear responses.

d. To begin the activity, bring out the pack of Self-Mastery Cards and spread them out in front of the group. Ask how many people have seen and used these cards? For many connected with Brahma Kumaris centers they know these cards very well. Each card has the name of a virtue with a description of it on it, and many of us use these in our meditation practice. We select a card each day, empowering the experience of the virtue in meditation, and then attend to the expression of the virtue by others and by the self throughout the day. It provides a nice spiritual focus for the day.

e. Let the group know that when exploring virtues it is really about exploring the energy of the soul. This energy resonates at different frequencies and is experienced in a multitude of ways by the soul and by others.

f. Tell people that rather than beginning with the names of virtues, we would like to begin the series by experimenting with discerning the energy of the soul, then attempting to give each vibrational tone a name. These descriptive names are known as virtues. To do this, we would like to begin with three experiments.

g. Have people sit in a circle (or if in large room – to look at a table at front). Place an object in the middle of the circle and ask the group to be silent and look at the object. Then ask them to close their eyes and go inside to check, detect and discern the energy they experience when looking at the object. Ask them to find names or words to describe the energy they experience after looking at the object and going inside. Place a variety of objects in the center of the circle on the floor or table. Sample objects can include something soft like an adorable stuffed animal that makes everyone go "ooohhh, aaahhh"; or a beautiful single flower (gerbera daisy or lily); and something hard but beautiful like a gong or Tibetan bowl.

h. After showing the first object, ask people to be in silence as they go inside and check. Then go around the circle - or if in a large group ask them to turn to their neighbor or in trios – and share words that describe the energy you feel inside when you look at the object.

i. Repeat this process three times until each object has provided a catalyst for the experience of one's internal energy.

j. Convene the full group again and have people share a word to describe the quality of energy they felt with each selected object.

k. Read Anthea Church's beautiful writing about virtue to the group.

l. State to the group that our understanding is that the energy of the 'being' or 'soul' is multi-faceted and we describe that energy with words, which we call virtues or values.

Each energy has a unique, distinct and subtle difference in how it feels. A standard feature each night throughout the virtue series will be to explore one of these energies or virtues and have a shared experience with it. Then at the end of the evening each one will summarize the energy by writing a brief summary on a business card. By collecting 26 virtue cards in their own plastic business card 8/11 sheet we will have a spiritual dictionary by the end of our 26 weeks!
30 minutes

Reflecting - What was the activity like for you – hearing about virtues, discerning energies, and giving them names? What was easy, familiar? What was difficult? What does this suggest about virtues generally?
10 minutes

Valuing the Experience - Hand out a business card and ask people to summarize their understanding of virtue on the card. Read aloud to share. Hear from each what they have written.
10 minutes

Embodying the Virtue – Ask everyone to select one of the virtue cards they are drawn to, or would like to have more of in their lives. During the following week, use this virtue as a focus for your intention when interacting with others. Observe this virtue in others and in yourself. Watch it grow.
End the session with silence or a song.
10 minutes

Resources and References - Materials required: blank business cards (one for each person), 3 objects ex. Soft toy, flower, gong; 8x11 plastic business card holders sheets (one for each person), *Today I Will Meditate on a Virtue* by Carmen Warrington on cd *Today I Will,* pack of Self-mastery Cards, *Inner Beauty* by Anthea Church

ACCURACY

Setting Intention - To explore what 'accuracy' feels and like looks like on my spiritual journey.

Meditation
20-30 minutes

Experiencing the Virtue - Exploring your spiritual aim.

a. Tell people the virtue for the evening. Ask them what accuracy might mean as a virtue. Hear responses. Many people say things like: arrow hitting the bulls eye target. Or knowing what is right and wrong. Doing the right thing, etc. Explore as they suggest ideas and capture the essence. Then suggest a definition from the self-mastery cards: As a master, I always consider each situation...knowing what to do, when to do it, and for exactly how long. I develop the instinct to recognize when something is not right and am ready to start over.

b. Ask people what they think of this.

c. Then ask them to stand up and in silence placing only their big toes on the ribbon to walk across the 'line' or tight wire of a ribbon stretched across the floor. (Have this ribbon about an inch wide laid across the carpet or tacked to the floor so it doesn't move - not long, maybe 4-5 feet).

d. Then everyone has crossed the line; ask them what was their experience? Listen to responses. Then ask what does this have to do with accuracy? Some do not see the connection. Some will see how focus and concentration help you be accurate. Ask them if they could feel themselves being accurate? Could they feel the virtue?

e. After some discussion, ask them how they know if they are being accurate? (Some people think accuracy is doing what others think is right) In the case of the ribbon, accuracy was staying on the line. Without a line, you don't know what accuracy is. Ask them, what is your line? What is the line you are attempting to walk in life? If you know that, then you will be able to tell if your daily actions/words are accurate (in line with that).

f.   Ask everyone to take a moment to consider what is their 'line' or in other words what is their spiritual aim? Perhaps give an example: my intention or aim in life is to be the most compassionate person I can be. Because this is my line, I can see where/when my actions/words have been in line with that or not. Without a clear sense of my line, I cannot know if I am being accurate.

g.   No need to share. Now hand out a small card to each one (see below) and ask them to identify 3 activities important for them to do everyday in order to stay true to that spiritual aim or to walk their line on a daily basis.

h.   After writing on their file cards, invite everyone to create a sequence of activities. We want you to image these activities as the steps in a dance sequence. When you know the dance, its natural and you flow through the steps accurately without effort. Like learning to salsa – there are a lot of 1-2-3 moves as you learn, and you repeat them until they flow together as a dance.

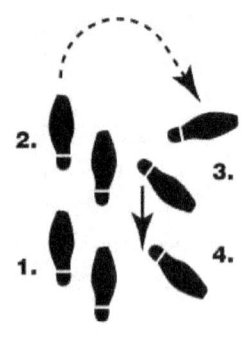

| **Life is a Dance**
Accuracy is the Steps
Identify 3 practical actions you need to
take every day in order to dance your
own dance - stay true to your aim.

1.

2.

3. |

i. Then ask each to stand up and position around the room facing outwards so you don't see anyone. Ask them to take the time to create an action to go with each of their three steps. For example, if one of my activities is to meditate everyday, I may hold my hands in front of me in the Namaste pose. Give them some time to figure it out.

j. Then tell them you would like them to make the movements as three steps in their daily dance of accuracy. And to repeat the sequence ten times as you play background music.

Play some happy music, and invite everyone to dance their steps of accuracy for about 5 min. Explain that repeating it physically will help them remember it and connect intention to action. The idea is to repeat the sequence of spiritual steps so that each one remembers what is important to do every day to remain accurate toward their spiritual aim. Dance until it becomes firm.
35 minutes

Reflecting - Ask people what the experience was like for them - from the beginning where you identified a spiritual aim, made your list, created a sequence and then danced it until it was yours. What was most significant? What did you learn?
10 minutes

Valuing the Experience – Ask people: what is your understanding of the virtue of accuracy now? Write on a business card and then share. Hear from all who wish to share.
5 minutes

Embodying the Virtue - This week begin each day with your dance to build your accuracy. Do it once more during the day, then at the end of the day check – did I dance my dance today and remain accurate on my path? Or did I have miss-steps when influenced by others? End the evening with a song.
10 minutes

Resources and References - Music Suggestions -*The Happy Song* by Will Pharell, *Return to* commentary from *Soul Consciousness: The Key to Freedom CD*. Paper and pens for writing, small cards with 3 steps and footprints, blank business cards

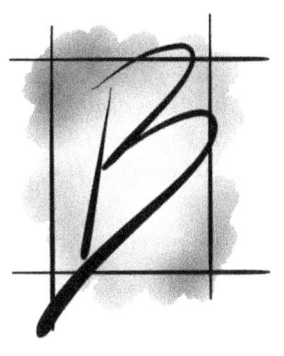

BENEVOLENCE

Setting Intention - To identify and learn about my button of benevolence.

Meditation
20-30 minutes

Experiencing the Virtue - This week the focus is benevolence.

a. Begin by showing a video clip. Explain that the video is called Eye to Eye and it is individuals (from Jewish and Muslim faiths) meeting eye to eye on camera. Ask people to watch in silence.

b. When the video is finished, hold the silence for a moment. Then ask people to check the feeling they have inside. How would you describe the feeling? Hear answers. Ask people what made this feeling emerge in them? What did they see/experience in the video that released this feeling? Hear answers.

c. Explain that tonight's virtue is benevolence. Ask people to share what they think benevolence is. Listen to comments and then share this reading from Anthea Church's book:

Benevolence is silent good will. It is like the sun shining on hard ground, softening the earth, melting the ice, but with no design or intention to heal. It is a state of naturalness, which is why it works because the ground feels no debt to the sun. In the same way, to be on the receiving end of benevolence is to be receiving something for which there is no return. Not even a pressure to respond-which is why one does, so easily.
Benevolence is a state of being, reliant on itself alone. It has nothing to do with feelings of mercy or preference, sudden stabs of love, it just is. It offers nothing specific, but everyone is drawn to it.

To have become benevolent is the best help you can be to anyone because benevolence has no shape, any more than sunlight has, but it can filter into the quiet corners of panic in a person's mind and lighten the burden. It is the least intrusive virtue and yet it is welcomed everywhere.

d. Share images or metaphors of benevolence. For example; when fruit is ripe it releases flavor in a rush when squeezed and eaten. An incense stick fills the atmosphere with fragrance that is unseen. Ask if anyone can think of another example. Ask if there are other examples?

e. Ask people to consider what is the button or catalyst that, when touched, releases this experience of silent good will? Share an example - on Christmas morning watching the kids open their presents is a time when the deep experience of benevolence is felt. Before there has been compassion, love, kindness, and generosity, but this feeling is unique and lasts a long time, needing nothing in return. Experiencing this good will is its own blissful state. What was the catalyst or button that released it? Seeing the innocent, pure happiness and joy spread on the faces of the children. Then ask everyone to think about this for a moment.

f. Pass out pink heart-shaped post it notes – and ask people to consider this their benevolence button. What is your benevolence button? Name it: what is the button that, when pushed, allows benevolence to flow out of you? Ask people to share their benevolence button and the story associated with it with the person next to them. Ask to hear some examples in the large group.

g. Add an idea about God. That God gets part of His reputation from the fact that benevolence is used often, sometimes almost exclusively, in connection with God. So what makes it so unique when in relation to God? Offer additional thoughts on the virtue such as 'God's benevolence never quits' - it is not momentary, not fleeting, doesn't change tomorrow, it is always there. Continue the discussion: what is the role and need for benevolence at this time in world? Hear suggestions from the group.

h. Now ask the group to consider how we can help sustain a consistent outpouring of good will in the world, through acts of benevolence. The core thought is probably their benevolence button, so put it in the center of the handout. What are the rays of energy that flow out from you when you see/remember this experience? And when you remember it now and each time you remember, you release this energy out to the world. Consider alone: write the feelings experienced on the rays of the circle extending out from your heart.

i. Now let us practice this in a couple moments of silence, using your mind:
   • Hold the core thought (benevolence button) clearly,
   • See how long you can sustain thinking about it clearly and releasing the feelings it brings for as long as possible,
   • Notice how it affects your experience of yourself.

j. Now ask people to stand up and move quietly and freely around the space for the next 2-3 minutes, holding the virtue of benevolence in their eyes, minds as they walk. Ask them to naturally and easily make eye contact with others without speaking and express this benevolence through the eyes.
   45 minutes

Reflecting - Ask the group to consider how they feel after being part of this activity? When finished, ask them how that was? Were they aware that they were spreading benevolence around like an incense stick that gives constant fragrance to the atmosphere. How do they feel now as compared to when they walked into the room? What does this suggest about benevolence? What does it suggest about how we can bring greater levels of benevolence into this needy world? Hear reflections from those who wish to share – ask if others had similar reflections.
10 minutes

Valuing the Experience - What did you learn about benevolence this evening, and how do you understand it now? Write your understanding on business card. Share in the group. *5 minutes*

Embodying the Virtue – Invite people to wear their benevolence button every other day this week and spread rays of that feeling. Experience and note the difference it makes. Close with a song. *5 minutes*

Resources and References - *Lightness of Being* from *Lights of World* meditation commentary CD.

YouTube clip: Eye to Eye
https://www.youtube.com/watch?v=ZMB3186v1nQ
Handout (on the next page), heart shaped post it notes, and pens.

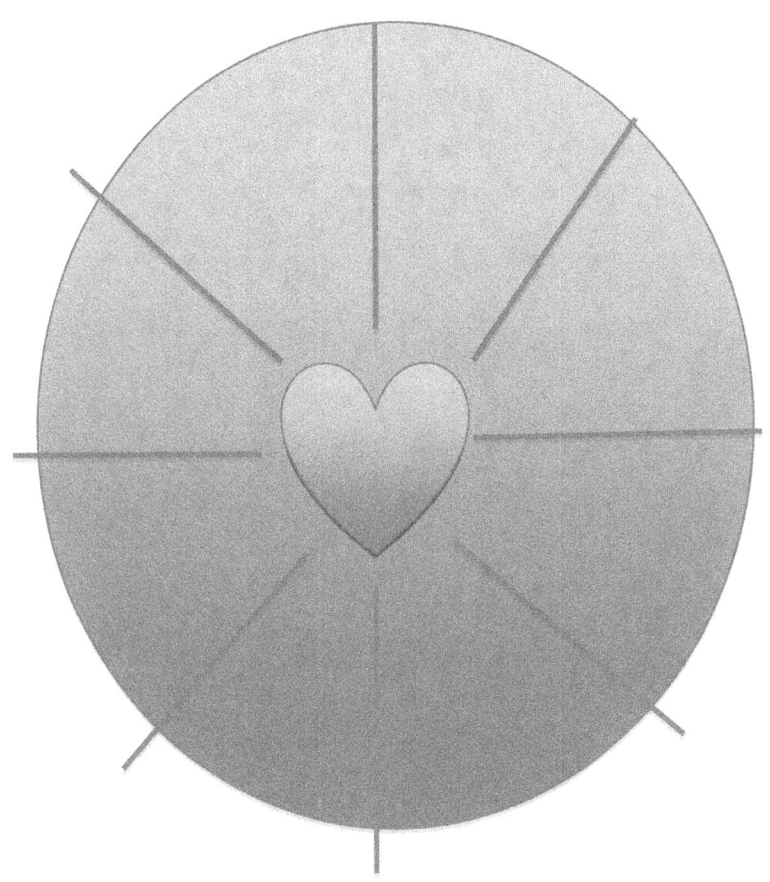

COOPERATION

Setting Intention - To explore giving and receiving cooperation.

Meditation
20-30 minutes

Experiencing the Virtue – Let the group know that in this session we will be exploring the virtue of cooperation. We will look at the giving and receiving of cooperation and its links to enthusiasm and courage.

a. Begin by exploring the group's experiences of cooperation by asking:
   - What does cooperation feel like and look like in your family, work, and community? Where does it come from, what is its source? What is its spiritual vibration?
   - Ask the group to share their initial thoughts with the person beside them.
   - Hear some examples in the big group.

b. Add to the group's descriptions of cooperation by explaining that this is the virtue that gets tasks done and accomplishes goals that could not be done by one person alone. Read from the cooperation self- mastery card:

   "The master has a quiet eye for what is needed to bring success. To supply it, at the right time, in the right place, and in a positive state of mind."

c. Let us brainstorm a few situations that require more than one person to complete. For example: celebrating a milestone birthday for someone in the family, or getting a new program in a community for people who require companionship or recreation. Now let us talk about examples of cooperative tasks in your world: what are 2-3 things that had to be done recently that required the help of others to do? The facilitator should have a handful of 8.5X11 paper and write one cooperative task, as suggested, in the center of each sheet of paper as they are offered.

d. Give the instructions for group work: Each group will get one or two sheets with one of the items mentioned in the brainstorming session. In your group discuss each one and identify the sources of cooperation that help get such a task done. What must a group of people bring to the table to get it done? Write these answers in the bottom left hand corner of the sheet of paper, below the task. Then in the upper right hand corner, identify what can be received as a result of having been part of the group that joined together to perform that specific cooperative task? Divide into trios, get your sheets and start sharing.

e. Have each trio share their results in the large group.
   35 minutes

Reflecting – Ask the group: what was that activity like for you? What feelings were brought up by your memories of cooperation and hearing examples from others? What does this tell us about what we know about cooperation? What can we learn from this discussion?
10 minutes

Valuing the Experience - Ask people to write their understanding of the virtue of cooperation on a business card and to share their answer with the group.
20 minutes

Embodying the Virtue – This week, look for tasks that require more than one person. Look for where you can give and receive cooperation. End with a song.
10 minutes

Resources and References - Sheets of paper, markers, music, inspiration from Mike George's *1001 Meditations* book page 502 – 290-291, the song *Lifted* by Bliss

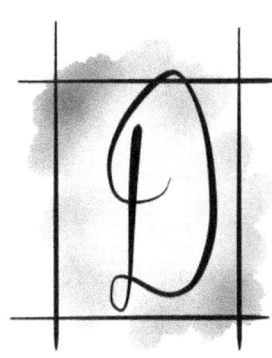

DISCIPLINE

Setting Intention - To explore the virtue of discipline.

Meditation
20-30 minutes

Experiencing the Virtue - Welcome all the participants to the session and give them an overview of the virtue series and its intention to increase our virtues literacy. Virtues are often inherent, hidden, or latent, and our spiritual journey often helps when we recognize them and bring them into being to enrich our lives. Tonight we will focus on the virtue of discipline. Read the description of discipline on the self-mastery card:

"I recognize the value of time and of effort. As a master I have the power to resist all forms of inertia."

a. Begin by asking the group what they think when they hear the word discipline? Some thoughts to start could include disciplining children, or the 12 disciples – called this because they lived a life based on Jesus' disciplines (as BK's we follow God's directions, called 'shrimat').

b. Continue the group conversation by moving to discussing discipline in the local society. What are symbols of discipline in this culture? Where is discipline understood and seen in this culture? How does it affect those who practice it, and those who have it practiced on them? What is the best form of discipline? In what areas of life would we wish to be more disciplined?

c. After hearing the group's answers, explain further what discipline is. For example, discipline refers to systematic instructions given to a learner that instructs the person to follow a particular code of conduct. For instance, in child development there are methods of modeling character and teaching self-control and acceptable behavior. Self–discipline, on the other hand, is training oneself to accomplish a task or add a particular pattern of behaviors to your personality so that you can be your best and behave your best, for your own well-being. Will power and self-control suggests that I will choose to do what is best and do it gladly, with a pure heart.

d. In this session we will use an Appreciative Inquiry (AI) approach to explore discipline. An AI approach has four questions that center on discovering, dreaming, designing, and doing. They are as follows:

First Question (Discover) - Ask everyone in the group to remember a time in their life when they made a promise to themselves (or someone else), which was for their own benefit? What helped you stay on track with this commitment? What benefits did you reap? Ask each one to think of their own answer and share it with the group. Afterwards, ask for a summary of the things people do to stay on track. Are there any common threads?

Second Question (Dream) - Ask the group members to consider what they want to do more of in their day for their own well-being. Ask everyone to stand up and in a circle, and like a clock, walk backwards or counterclockwise through the day that has just passed.

Have them consider what thoughts, things, and people they thought about. Make a list of them all. Afterwards, pass the lists around until everyone has someone else's list.

Get them to pretend they are a good friend of the person, and have them review the list and code it by placing a heart, question mark or X next to each activity on the list. Base this on the following:

- For thoughts, etc. that are considered good for a soul.

? - For thoughts, etc. considered neutral – neither good nor bad for a soul.

X - For thoughts, etc. that are considered bad for a soul.

Third Question (Design) - Return the lists to their owners. Have them look at their lists and consider what they would like to do to practice using discipline this week. What is something on their list of thoughts they would like to reduce, recycle, renew, retire, or replace. Ask them to choose one item that will allow them to practice discipline. Have them decide how they will go about this: what reminders will help them with their new discipline?

Fourth Question (Do) - Ask everyone in the group to consider what they will do next week to practice discipline in one area. This isn't easy – show a little video to demonstrate how difficult it can be. But we can all get very serious about our ability to bring discipline into our lives. Show this video of the marshmallow test to help put things into perspective:
http://www.youtube.com/watch?v=QX_oy9614HQ

Before the session, watch this explanation of the background to the test. No need to show this clip during the session, just explain it to the participants:
http://www.youtube.com/watch?v=xNvvL9j_SIs&feature=related

e. Lay out little pieces of glass or stone (enough for each person). Have each person choose a piece of glass as a touchstone to help in maintaining discipline and keeping their promise to themselves this week.
50-60 minutes

Reflecting – Ask the group what the experience of the evening was like for them. What part did they find most revealing about their own relationship with discipline? What does this suggest to you about discipline? What do others think about that? Was everyone's experience similar? If not, what were the differences?
10 minutes

Valuing the Experience – Ask the group what their understanding of discipline is now after the session. What other virtues does it call into play? Have each of them write a summary of what discipline means to them on a business card. Hear everyone's answer.
10 minutes

Embodying the Virtue - Ask each participant to pick one thing they will do with discipline this week for their own good (and do it gladly!). Close with silence for a moment or play an uplifting song.
5 minutes

Resources and References - Paper, pens, projector, computer, the Internet, the Marshmallow Test video -
http://www.youtube.com/watch?v=QX_oy9614HQ,
http://www.youtube.com/watch?v=xNvvL9j_SIs&feature=related,
And touchstones (pieces of polished rock or glass).

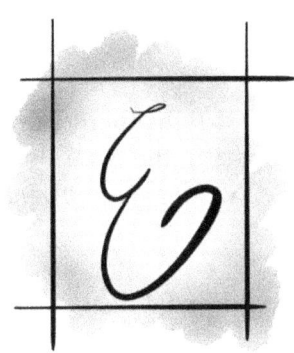

ENTHUSIASM

Setting Intention - To (re) ignite our enthusiasm.

Meditation
20-30 minutes

Experiencing the Virtue – Welcome the group, and check-in on how last week's homework went. Introduce enthusiasm as the virtue for this week. Enthusiasm comes easily when one is well stocked in the energy of positive thoughts and feelings (joie de vivre).

a. To begin, we're going to watch a short video. Ask the group to track their feelings on a piece of paper while they watch it. Once everyone is ready, show the video 'Enlightening Ride on Subway': https://www.youtube.com/watch?v=xmDFt7Obz2U

b. Ask everyone to think about what positive thoughts and feelings were lit inside of them while watching the video. Name these qualities and place them as stars on the handout paper.

c. Next ask the group to take a moment to reflect on what ignites this joie de vivre in them. Perhaps provide commentary of being 'lit up from the inside out'.

d. Offer a basket of tea lights and ask each person to take a candle for each positive thought or quality that they have experienced being lit inside them recently (if there are more than 5 people ask them to take a candle for the top 2 or 3).

e. Ask each person in turn to light a candle and name the quality they felt. Place the candle on a prepared tabletop or platform until all the lit candles have been added and table is full of lit candles.

f. Next, ask each person to take sparklers and light them from these candles. Dance around the room with the sparklers while playing a happy song (for example *Walking on Sunshine* by Katrina and the Waves).

g. Share a definition of enthusiasm from the original Greek word 'Entheos'. It means having God within. Read from the self-mastery card:

"As a master, I see the fulfillment of my destiny clearly. Success is my right and my eyes do not stray to the temporary setbacks along the way."

h. Read from Dadi Janki's book, 'Inside Out' (page 33-34):

"When we draw on positive qualities such as peace, happiness, acceptance and kindness this experience is the oil that primes our lamps. It creates a link with God. The reason is that we share these qualities with God. When you make these preparations all that remains is to kindle the light inside with a spark of love. This can come automatically and you narrow the gap between God and yourself. Then the energy flows. This is an amazing wonderful thing. It's as if within the flame, there is the fuel that makes the light shine brightly. It shows in your eyes, on your face, and it comes through in your actions. It lightens up others, too."

h. Ask people to take a moment to consider how they can keep these qualities of God lit within them.
45 minutes

Reflecting - Ask the group to think about and share their thoughts on what the experience of enthusiasm was like for them tonight (the video, the activity, the definitions, etc.)? What does it suggest to us about enthusiasm?
10 minutes

Valuing the Experience – Ask the group what they understand about enthusiasm from our shared experience and conversation tonight. Have them write their summary on their business card. Share with the group.
10 minutes

Embodying the Virtue - This week take 5 minutes once per day to light your candle of enthusiasm! Play the song from before again to end the evening.
5 minutes

Resources and References - Video set-up, paper, pens, stick-on stars, candle handout, candles, sparklers. The *Absorb and Emit Light* commentary from *Lights of the World* CD as part of meditation; the laughing Yogi video
(https://www.youtube.com/watch?v=xmDFt7Obz2U).

Music: *A Beautiful Day* – Bill Withers, *Walking on Sunshine* by Katrina and the Waves

ENTHUSIASM HANDOUT
Entheos = To Have God within

"As a master, I see the fulfillment of my destiny clearly. Success is my right and my eyes do not stray to the temporary setbacks along the way."

Positive thoughts or feelings while watching the video:

FEARLESSNESS

Setting Intention - To explore the virtue of fearlessness.

*As preparation for the session, lay a big yellow ribbon around the room, creating a circle of protection that all people can enter and sit within.

Meditation – Play the *Wizard* commentary from *Relax Kids*. *20-30 minutes*

Experiencing the Virtue – Introduce the session by asking the group to sit inside the circle laid out on the floor. Announce to them that they have entered the golden circle of protection for this session. Explain that in this circle fear cannot exist. Accordingly, in this session we are exploring the topic of fearlessness.

a. Start by suggesting that at this time even talking about fearlessness is bold, given how much fear there is in the world. Fear is like a corset we are all wearing that at times gets pulled tighter and tighter, to the point that it even impedes our breathing, etc. For some of us fear is like wallpaper – it is the backdrop we are no longer even aware of, but it affects our actions and thoughts in such a way that we limit ourselves by withholding and shrinking away.
   - Ask the group: what is fear anyway?

b. After hearing their answers, offer this explanation: fear can be defined as the emotional and physiological response I have to something I perceive as a threat to my security.
   - Ask: what would it be like to be so profoundly secure that nothing could threaten me? Let us consider this for a moment in silence. Hear responses.

c. Next, tell three stories about fearlessness to depict the three principles behind fearlessness. Each principle is effective in creating a space between the self and fear - i.e. loosening the corset. It is in this space that one can experience fearlessness.

The principles are as follows:
- **Hold a pure intention** - Recognize where you have built your sense of security on temporary supports. The first of these supports is the physical body; the second is on other people, situations, etc. When I practice experiencing myself as a soul - as being bodiless - there is no fear.
- **Transform your vision of the situation** - By transforming the way you see a situation, you are taking the threat out of it and instead seeing opportunity for benefit. This approach is described in the book *Four Faces of Woman* by Caroline Ward (page 229 - a story of transforming fear).
- **Switch on the awareness of my powerful stage of the soul** - Remember that you are bodiless and indestructible. Nothing can destroy energy. Say this in silence to yourself six times: "I am a body. I have a soul." Check the effect this has - how does it make you feel? Then switch the thought around and instead say six times "I am a soul, I have a body". Check the effect of this. Ask the group to share their thoughts.

d. Now that the three principles have been named, help the group play with them by using the commentary below. Ask the group to sit in silence, and read the following to them:

"Establish yourself in the soul conscious stage. Say to yourself: 'I am not the body'. Pull in the power of soul that is being extended outwards through the tendril of thought to other people, situations, places, and events. Let me pull in all of this power and concentrate it at its source: I, the soul. This is the switch of powerful awareness. I am completely secure in my starting point as I enter this meditation. I will hold this awareness as consistently as I can throughout this visualization."

"Now, imagine yourself moving through a day, or that you are in a serene situation. In this situation you meet a source of fear for you - imagine the presence of something that provokes a fear response. Now STOP – in this moment be the detached observer and take note of the feelings and physical reactions you are having as you encounter this source of fear. Now make contact again, and see how this fear in your mind manifests practically in the situation unfolding in front of you. Take note of the recognizable factors and expressions within the situation."

"Again, STOP. Pull back and detach and observe the situation. Check and clarify the purity of your intention. Now re-engage with the situation with your pure intention as protection. Witness what happens when you do this. Now pull back and take note of anything that happened in the situation. "

"Re-engage and bring your reframe to transform the situation. Take note of anything that came up as protection during that interaction as you faced the fear that has taken up residence in your mind. Now come back to the room."

e. Ask everyone to turn around and face outside the circle after the commentary. Ask them to imagine that they are completely safe inside the circle, the entire group has 'their back' and look outside the circle to imagine what causes them fear, knowing they are safe, they are powerful, and nothing can touch them.

f. Have the group share points of fearlessness that they experienced in the situation.

g. Ask each person to consider what sustains this circle of protection for them. What fills the circle with power? Write this on a piece of golden ribbon and put it on as a bracelet.

h. Gently invite people to step out of the physical circle of protection but take the feeling of it with them inside of themselves.
45 minutes

Reflecting – Ask the group what the experience of exploring fearlessness was like for them. From definitions, thought experiments, and sitting in the circle of protection - what were their thoughts and feelings through the activity? What does this suggest about fearlessness?
10 minutes

Valuing the Experience Ask the group to consider their understanding of fearlessness and to write their answers on business cards and share with the group.
10 minutes

Embodying the Virtue – For homework, ask the group to wear their bracelets of protection and remember to call on the virtue of fearlessness when needed throughout this week. Play a closing song or sit in silence.
5 minutes

Resources and References – A very long piece of golden or yellow ribbon, pieces of golden ribbon that you can write on to use as bracelets, stories of fearlessness from *Four Faces of Woman* book by Caroline Ward, *Relax Kids - Wizards* meditations commentary CD.

GENTLENESS

Setting Intention - To explore my own virtue of gentleness.

Meditation – Include the *Spirit of Innocence* from Carmen Warrington's *Healing Heart and Soul* CD.
20-30 minutes

Experiencing the Virtue – Welcome everyone and introduce them to the virtue of Gentleness. Begin by exploring the virtue:

a. Start by having magazine cut outs in the center of the group – either on a table or on the floor. Ask the participants to start by identifying images from the pictures that represent them at their best. Next, ask them to pick one picture that depicts them when they are at their gentlest (i.e. you at your 'gentle best').

b. Ask everyone to identify some key words to describe their gentlest state, and/or depict what it feels like inside with a gesture. As the facilitator, write down words you hear to depict experience/expression of gentleness (to be used later).

c. To describe gentleness find a very delicate object (we used a gold painted leaf). Have the group touch the leaf without breaking it. Suggest that gentleness is about leaving no impact, for example, to take something very delicate, like a gold leaf, and to hold it without breaking it. Continue to demonstrate with the leaf while you share the following ideas about gentleness:

> *"Gentleness is a quality that does not disturb, doesn't push, yet knows its power and can provide shelter. Real gentleness in a person is a great power. The power that sees, understands, but never interferes. Like the branch of a tree, just touching the earth but never taking root in it. Never to take root in someone else's mind but to help - that's gentleness."*

From the self-mastery card:

> " I stay close to my feelings of myself. So quiet, so sensitive to the feelings of others - as a master, I can never hurt someone's feelings due to being out of touch with my own. To walk the earth and leave no trace – no harsh evidence of having been there – spoilage, rubbish, etc."

d. Now tell the group we will look at the physical level - let us see what it takes to leave no impact. Ask everyone to get up and walk on the carpet and see if they can cross the room without leaving an impact/indent on the carpet. After everyone has tried it, ask:

- What did that activity take?
- What did you notice happening inside of you as you attempted to leave no impact?

e. Another form of gentleness can be found in a form of poetry called 'Haiku'. Haikus demonstrate the low impact nature of gentleness. To create a haiku requires being so quiet and internally focused that all that is necessary is a few words, spoken sparingly. Read the following sample haikus to depict the experience of gentleness.

Two birds on the branch
Soft tree balanced dancing
Never to take root

Gentle thoughts and words
Produce good fruit

Emerging life
Dancing with the light
Expressed joie de vivre

Peaceful positive energy
Bending contradictions
With lightness

Delicate, tender
Soft aliveness of love,
Home

Delicate to me
Never seen by you or me
But felt in the deepest way

f. Now knowing what this gentle form of poetry sounds like, you may also want to know what it looks like – it follows a simple rule 5-7-5 i.e. 5 syllables in the first line, 7 syllables in the next and 5 in the last. Ask everyone to begin writing their own haiku as a practice of 'gentleness'. Give everyone the handout found on the next page, and allow people to sit quietly and create their own haiku.

g.   Once everyone has had enough time, ask them to read their haiku out loud. Clap gently for each or use the American Sign Language form of clapping, which is to wave your hands above your head without sound.
30 minutes

Reflecting – Ask the group to consider what they noticed about gentleness as they moved through the exercises with the magazines, the readings and the haikus. Ask them what helped them get in touch with gentleness. What did they notice about themselves as they did each activity? What does it suggest to them about gentleness?
10 minutes

Valuing the Experience – Ask the group to write their own understanding of gentleness on a business card and share with the group.
10 minutes

Embodying the Virtue - Take your gentle self to work this week and watch what happens around you. End the evening with a closing song or silence.
10 minutes

Resources and References – A variety of magazine cut outs, fragile golden leaf decoration or other very delicate object, paper, pens, haiku handouts, music from the *Healing Heart and Soul* CD.

HAIKU HANDOUT

"Nothing is so strong as gentleness and nothing is so gentle as real strength."
–Ralph W. Sockman

"Only the weak are cruel. Gentleness can only be expected from the strong."
-    Leo Buscaglia

"When you encounter difficulties and contradictions, do not try to break them, but bend them with gentleness and time."
-    Saint Francis de Sales

"Gentleness corrects whatever is offensive in our manner."
-Hugh Blair

A Haiku is 5,7,5 syllables per line OR up to 17 syllables

reflected
in the rushing brook - how still the white
magnolia

HUMILITY

Setting Intention - To explore the experience of humility, and to understand that our spiritual journey is bringing each of us 'our lessons' providing all that is needed for each one to learn their own lessons.

Meditation – Include *Release Into Peace* commentary from the *Today I Will* CD by Carmen Warrington.
20-30 minutes

Experiencing the Virtue - Welcome the group and let them know that the virtue you will be exploring this week is humility. Tell the group you would like to jump right into an activity to explore humility, with their permission. Ask: is everyone ok with that? If anyone has comments from last week's experience or questions for this session, listen and respond without revealing the nature of the upcoming activity. Once all comments have been heard, begin the activity:

a. Offer everyone a piece of clean white paper. Ask them to think of a situation they know of where someone needed help. On the piece of paper, draw the scenario with the person needing help or assistance at the center of the page. Ask them to draw all the people involved in the situation around that person. Place those most closely connected to trying to help the person near the center and those who are contributing less directly to the situation, but are still involved in some way, around the edges. Be sure to include yourself.

b. Next, ask people to take a different coloured pencil and draw arrows towards the person needing help, if the supporters are directly helping, use a solid line; if they are less involved use a dotted or broken line. Connect everyone in the picture to the person needing help.

c. Then ask everyone to select another coloured pencil and now create a new set of arrows in which every person in the image has a line connected to YOU. You are now the central figure, NOT the person who needed help. Draw every line as a solid line.

d. Suggest to the group: this is now a very different picture. Have them look at their picture and ask them what they feel looking at that? What stands out for them? Hear answers, reactions. Often people feel overwhelmed, responsible, etc.

e. Now ask them to reflect in silence for a moment by explaining: Think of all the people in the scene as actors in your very personal drama. Each of these people has come together into this very complex situation in order to help YOU learn a specific lesson. The situation has been carefully orchestrated like a play in order to bring out qualities, powers and virtues in YOU, that could only be brought out in this way. With this in mind - ask people to consider the scenario with the arrows coming towards them and reflect on the lesson they might be learning from each person. What is the situation asking you to pay attention to, to learn about for your own growth? What is the lesson, blessing, or virtues/powers the situation is developing in them?

f. Next ask each person to name the scene – this is the story of _____(your own name) learning the lesson of _____ (the power, virtue, inner quality). And then to begin writing the story in the third person. When she ... then she... and this helped her learn about... etc. write for 5 minutes without lifting your pen from the paper. At the end add your appreciations to everyone in the scene.

g. Have people in the group read what they have written to themselves so that everyone can appreciate what others are learning.

h. Finally, read the definition of humility from the self-mastery cards:

"I am the master who is unmasked. I see that the reality is that my gifts and talents aren't mine. I hold them in trust for the benefit of the world. As a master, I no longer need to prove myself."
30 minutes

Reflecting – Ask the group what the experience of the exercise was like for them. What did they experience as they redirected the arrows? What did they feel like as they looked at the two scenes? What does this suggest about humility?
10 minutes

Valuing the Experience – Ask: what does humility mean to you? Have them write their answers on a business card and share it in the group.
5 minutes

Embodying the Virtue – Suggest to the group that in the upcoming week they should allow the situations they are in and the people they are with to be their teachers. Be humble. Note how they feel each time they are aware that the situation is set up for them to learn. End the evening with a closing song
5 minutes

Resources and References - Paper, coloured pencils (three different colours for each person), music – the *Release Into Peace* commentary from the *Today I Will* CD by Carmen Warrington.

INTROVERSION

Setting Intention - To move inside ourselves and practice the virtue of introversion.

Meditation – Include *Stepping Inwards* commentary by Anthony Strano.
20-30 minutes

Experiencing the Virtue - Welcome everyone to the session and let them know that the focus for the evening is on the virtue of 'Introversion'. Ask them: what comes to mind when you think of this virtue? Listen to their responses. Often there is confusion in thinking about introversion associated with being anti-social.

a. After some sharing, offer the Hindi understanding of introversion, which is to turn the face within. Read the description of the virtue from the self-mastery cards:

> *"As a master, I turn to my inner realms, where my original qualities of peace, love and well-being reside. I see the inner meaning of my existence, the purpose of my life and I am content."*

Share that meditation is about 'going deep into the well'...or into the rooms of my inner house to discover something deep and eternal within the self.

b. Let them know that we will experiment with introversion in this session. To continue, take a few moments in meditation to go within. Use a commentary to guide them:

> *I allow my body to relax,*
> *Breathing naturally and easily.*
> *I settle into inner silence,*
> *Alone with myself.*
> *I touch the core of my being,*
> *The pulse of peace,*
> *My essence.*

I use the power of my imagination,

And mind to detect an inner treasure chest,
Full of positive qualities, and jewels of wisdom.
I enjoy the experience of being deep inside my own mind,
Enjoying the discovery of such riches.
I take a moment to consider what beauty and wisdom and depth
There is at the core of my being.
I let myself put words to these discoveries

c. Gently ask the group to return their awareness to this room and the sound of the voice that was guiding them.
Ask each participant to take one of the very little pieces of paper and write their answers to the following statement: "At the core of my being is..." Ask them to draw on what they discovered during the meditation to finish the statement – i.e. what gems did they discover within themselves?

d. When everyone has finished writing, pass around a basket of straws (cut into one inch lengths), balloons, and a small length of string/ribbon. Ask each person to take one of each. Then ask everyone to roll up their piece of paper and squeeze it into the end of the straw, and then place it gently into the balloon.

e. Next, ask everyone to blow up their balloon and tie it gently without knotting the string.

f. Then ask everyone to get up and move around. As they do so, toss the balloons all around the room. After a few minutes of fun, ask people to select a balloon that is not their own.

g. When everyone is seated with a balloon, ask them to take five full minutes alone and in silence to consider how to go inwards to get to the wisdom that is buried deep within that balloon. At a certain point, they should do whatever they need to discover the message hidden within. Once everyone has their message – whether done easily or with difficulty, (with violence or non-violence) ask them to take another few moments of silence to contemplate the message.

h. Hear some of the messages from inside the balloons. If a small group, hear from each person.
45 minutes

Reflecting – Take a few moments to reflect on the whole experience, considering your thoughts of your inner self, of preparing your balloon, and then getting another person's balloon. Remember your initial thoughts and feelings when asked to get inside the balloon:
- What were you thinking/feeling?
- What approach did you take to get inside the balloon?

Hear a variety of experiences. Now ask them to compare this experience of getting inside the balloon to their own approach to getting inside themselves. How do they approach going inside and discovering the messages or wisdom stored there? What insights can be taken from this experience about going within?
15 minutes

Valuing the Experience – Ask everyone to take a business card and write their understanding of introversion on it. Hear what people wrote about introversion.
10 minutes

Embodying the Virtue – Think about the upcoming week and ask the participants to choose a time when they can practice introversion. Preferably they would practice it at the same time every day for 5-15 min. Ask them to notice the benefits that they experience by doing this. End the evening with a song/silence and closure.
10 minutes

Resources and references - one balloon per person, small pieces of paper, 1 inch length of drinking straw, wrapping ribbon or string, pens; *Stepping Inwards* (Anthony Strano)

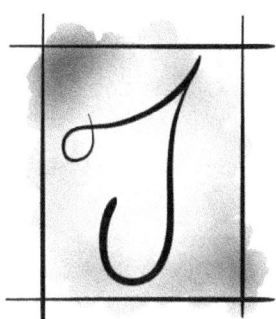

JOY

Setting Intention - To reconnect with our natural state of joy.

Meditation – Include the commentary *Inner Sanctuary* by Carmen Warrington. *20-30 minutes*

Experiencing the Virtue - Welcome everyone to the session on Joy. Introduce the virtue through some quotes:

"He who binds to himself a joy does winged flight destroy, but he who kisses the joy as it flies lives in eternity's sunrise."
-William Blake

"I am at play in the world; everything that I experience fills me with delight. My greatest pleasure lies in sharing and spreading joy."
-Khalil Gibran

"Forget not the earth delights to feel your bare feet and the wind longs to play with your hair."
–Khalil Gibran

a. Ask people to get comfortable and lead them through a commentary:

"Imagine a picture of yourself, laughing, smiling, and bubbling over with joy. Capture that moment and allow the positive feelings to seep into your present awareness. Expand the feeling as much as possible by visualizing all that was around you at that time. Bask in the warmth generated by these memories. Return your focus to the present moment bringing your sense of joy with you."

b. With a partner, share what the moment of joy was during the commentary and the feelings associated with it.

c. Next, play *Walking on Sunshine* by Katrina and the Waves for group to hear. Then get the participants into group of three or four. Tell them to share their joy stories with each other. From there, create two lines for the song they just listened to, using elements from their stories. Hear the music again while each group is working so they can work on their rhythm and cadence.

d.   When everyone is ready, arrange the sequence in which the groups will go, creating a collective song with all of their lyrics. Turn off the music and let each group sing their part, with everyone joining together to sing the chorus. Have bubble makers ready to make bubbles and blow in the room while the group sings.
40 minutes

Reflecting – Ask the group to share how they felt about the experience. Lead the group in thoughts about the experience of hearing about joy, doing the meditation, and preparing their lines for the song. Ask: what did you 'en-joy' about that experience? What was appealing about the experience? What does it suggest about creating joy or joy-full moments?
10 minutes

Valuing the Experience – Ask the group to consider what stands out for them about joy from their experiences this evening. Have them write their answers on business cards and share them with the group.
10 minutes

Embodying the Virtue - Give your joy to others this week. Give it for free, with no reason for it other than to just be and to give! Play with this virtue. Close the evening by playing *Walking on Sunshine* one last time.
10 minutes

Resources and References – Music: *Walking on Sunshine* by Katrina and the Waves and *Inner Sanctuary* by Carmen Warrington. Pens and paper bubble making sets.

KNOWING

Setting Intention - To explore the sources and roots of knowledge needed to transform the world.

Meditation – Include a commentary of your choice.
20-30 minutes

Experiencing the Virtue – Check-in with the group regarding the last session – hear how their week went. Introduce tonight's session by letting them KNOW that it will be about becoming researchers, exploring what we already know about helping transform the world. Suggest that often information out there cannot be trusted, but rather our own internal feelings or instincts of what is happening around us. Using this we can discern what is real and what is not. Ask the group in a playful way: 'are you ready to become researchers?'

a. The first step in any good research project is formulating your specific research question – i.e. what is something you would like to know about that will help transform the world? Take a moment to create a question individually.

b. Once they have their questions, hand out the research form (found below). Invite souls to move around the group and conduct a series of at least five individual interviews in the next 15 minutes using their research questions. Know that you will also be a contributor to the research of others.

c. After five minutes, invite souls into silence and ask them to consider the bits of data they collected in the form of opinions and ideas. Discuss how this raw data can contain patterns when it is analyzed to discover threads and themes. So now that the interviews are finished, have everyone sit with their data. Ask them to look at isolated bits they collected from each person, and then summarize the data into some emerging themes. Ask themselves: what is similar and what is different/dissimilar in the information?

d. Next, suggest that information becomes knowledge when we consider what the information is suggesting about your question. What knowledge is emerging from the information you have summarized? Where have you heard this sort of thing before, either affirmed or rejected? Take a moment to consider.

e. Ask the group to sit in meditation with their highest authority (God) and present their questions and the data and information they gathered to God. What feels right to you? Listen and intuit a response. Ask them to share what they discovered in small groups or pairs.

f. Ask the group: based on your research and reflection, what do you know will help transform the world? Have individuals share their conclusions.
45 minutes

Reflecting Ask: what was the experience of being a researcher like for you? What did you notice about the process we used? What does this tell you about your own data and information? How can this help you on your spiritual journey?
10 minutes

Valuing the Experience – Ask the group: what do you understand about knowledge from tonight's research experience? Have them write a definition on a business card. Have them share their answers with the group.
10 minutes

Embodying the Virtue – During the next week, ask the group to do their own research into a spiritual matter that is important to each of them. Have them interview people around them as well as exploring the work of others on the same theme. Close the evening with an uplifting song (suggestion: *When You Know* by Shawn Colvin).

5 minutes

Resources and References - Copy of the research form for each person, pens.

Music: *Here and Now* by Christine Sullivan, and *When You Know* *by* Shawn Colvin
(https://www.youtube.com/watch?v=SXJ8FPGUv7Q).

Research Form

The question I would like to ask others about transforming the world is:

Name of person asked	What they said (Data)	Summary of what was said (Information)	What it suggests/means to me (Knowledge)

Based on my research, one thing I know to be true is:

Date: Signed:

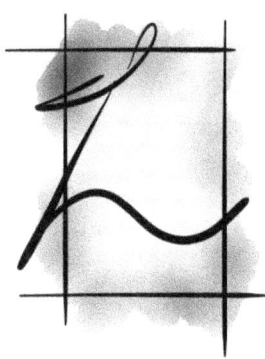

LIBERATION

Setting Intention - To explore strategies for liberation in the face of what life's drama throws at us.

Meditation - With suggested commentary: *Simply Let Go* by Carmen Warrington on the *Today I Will* CD. *20-30 minutes*

Experiencing the Virtue - Welcome the group members and check-in on last week's experience of embodying the virtue of knowing. Once they have shared their experiences, introduce the virtue for tonight's session: liberation.

a. Start with a brief commentary focusing on 'the best you':

"Take a moment and imagine your perfect self – the soul that is you – having done all the work to be the best you can be. What kind of body would suit you? What kind of being would best express the soul that is you?"
With that image firmly in your mind, return to this room.

b. Ask the group to think about one barrier/obstacle they are experiencing at this time. It could be something in what they think, say, or do that separates them from their perfect self. Give them strips of paper – cut 8 ½ X 11 into 6 strips lengthwise - and ask them to write each obstacle in big letters on a strip of paper (one obstacle per strip).

c. Next create a chain of barriers by taping the ends of one strip of paper with an obstacle written on it together into a loop. Then ask each person to loop their obstacle through the previous one, while telling the others about this obstacle that prevents them from being their best self. Once all the obstacles are attached as a paper chain, name it 'the chain that limits us from being who we truly are'.

d. Discuss what the word 'chain' suggests. What are the positive and negative connotations of the word? Whatever the connotation, it is clear that chains can constrain and we must loosen or remove these chains in order to move freely.

e. On a flipchart demonstrate two cycles:
    • **Vicious Thoughts** – These lead to feeling bad, saying bad things, and acting bad.
    • **Virtuous Cycle** – This leads to thinking good thoughts, feeling good, speaking well of others, and behaving well.
    Continue with the idea that we can break out of the Vicious Cycle anywhere to begin a new Virtuous Cycle. This is what liberation is about – bringing the positive into your life.

f. Ask the group to look at our 'chain that limits us'. Get them to identify where we can break into this vicious chain/cycle to create a virtuous cycle.

g. Read out some of the vicious thoughts on the chain and ask for suggestions/strategies that could loosen, remove, and/or replace these chains. Ask the group to brainstorm and generate ideas for each one and for the person who wrote it to listen.

h. After reading out several examples of the chain links and generating strategies, ask the group "what would happen to this chain, to our relationships, and to us if we used these strategies? "
    45 minutes

Reflecting – Ask the group to consider and share some of their thoughts and feelings they experienced as they worked through that activity on liberation. Ask them to review their experience from the 'best me' meditation, to the obstacles, to making the chain, to hearing about vicious and virtuous cycles, and to generating 'breakthrough strategies', what was most helpful to them. What insights do they now have about liberation? Have

them share their thoughts in the group.
15 minutes

Valuing the Experience – Ask: what do this evening's activities suggest to you about liberation? Have them write their understanding on a business card, to be read out loud.
10 minutes

Embodying the Virtue – Suggest to the group that they pick one strategy from tonight which they know they could use this week in one area of their life to liberate them from a place where they feel caught in a vicious cycle. End with silence or a song (suggestion: *Be Who You Were Born To Be* by Bliss).
5 minutes

Resources and References – Music: *Simply Let Go* by Carmen Warrington from the *Today I Will* CD, *Be Who You Were Born To Be* by Bliss. Strips of colored paper, markers and glue sticks or stapler to make the paper chain.

MATURITY

Setting Intention - To reveal how we carry maturity with us throughout our lives and use it to face difficult situations.

Meditation - With the suggested Commentary of *Calm Perspective* by Carmen Warrington on the *Today I Will* CD.
20-30 minutes

Experiencing the Virtue – Check-in with the group on their experiences from the last session. Once they have shared, introduce that this session will be about the virtue of maturity.

a. Ask people what comes to mind when they think of maturity. Hear responses.

b. Then read the self-mastery card for maturity:

> *"I am unaffected by surprises. I know the ways of the world. I have gone beyond displaying my ego. I take care of the reputation of others."*

Ask people what they understand from this.

c. Offer people the idea that things mature over time. Just like fruit ripens over time and there comes a moment when it is perfect to eat. Before then when it is not ripe, it is premature to eat it. What happens if you eat unripe fruit?

d. Suggest that in the same way, people mature over time AND situations also mature over time. Invite the group to remember if they have experienced times when they faced circumstances or a situation where they thought, "Oh my god, will this never end!' Or "Why is this happening to me?" Some time later they could look back on it and say with some equanimity: "I know that was bad, but if it hadn't happened I would never have known or learnt about ____."

e. Give each person a file card. Ask them to write down a description of such a situation that they have experienced, where, at the time it was difficult and seemed terrible, but in retrospect it had a purpose. Have them describe this on the file card (do not write their later realization on the cards – only write the difficult situation). Please choose one that has been resolved that you can look at in the past and see the benefit.

f. Deposit all the file cards in a basket. Next, have each person choose a card that is not their own and read it to themselves. Then, one by one, have them offer from a place of maturity something that they think a person might have learnt or gained insight into from such an experience. The purpose of this activity is for the group to act as a spiritual resource to each person, as we explore the silver linings in the past and future of such a scenario. Ask each person to listen anonymously when their card is being read.

Hear each situation (of if the group is large have them share in pairs with the person sitting next to them) and allow time for suggestions of lessons and silver linings. Take a few minutes for each one. The intention is to reveal the maturity within us as we look at situations with perspective and wisdom.

g. Wrap up the discussion with the line from the movie ' *The Best Exotic Marigold Hotel*': "Everything will be all right in the end. If it is not all right, then it is not yet the end." In other words we have not yet seen the 'all rightness' of the situations. Maturity can be holding the awareness that every situation will mature over time and that it will be okay in the end. In this way I am spared from reacting prematurely to judge a situation until it has had time to mature.
30 minutes

Reflecting - Lead the group in a reflection. Ask: what stood out for you during this activity? What does it suggest to you about the virtue of maturity? What insights did you have? Have them share with the group.
10 minutes

Valuing the Experience – Ask: what does this evening's experience suggest to you about the virtue of maturity? Have them write their answers on a business card. Share the answers in the group.
10 minutes

Embodying the Virtue – Instruct the group to take time this week to look at difficult situations with an eye to the past and the future. With maturity, relax in the awareness that "this too shall pass". End the evening with an uplifting song (Suggestion: *It's a Wonderful World* by Louis Armstrong).
10 minutes

Resources and References - *Calm Perspective* commentary by Carmen Warrington on the *Today I Will* CD, *It's a Wonderful World* by Louis Armstrong, file cards.

NEWNESS

Setting Intention - To explore the virtue of newness and ways to introduce newness into my life.

There are many connotations of newness, both big and small, in our daily lives. When we think of making a fresh start it is with anticipation, mixed with nervousness. Yet we still want to explore possibilities, to clean our slate, to be adventurous and open, and to allow excitement to take us further than we would normally go.

Meditation - Include a commentary of your choice. *20-30 minutes*

Experiencing the Virtue – This evening will be about exploring approaches to creating newness. Invite participants to consider what they do to create a feeling of newness in their lives. Consider examples of external changes we make in a consumer-oriented world. These include: buying something new to wear, changing our style, getting new music or finding a new restaurant to frequent.

a. Invite people to write down a short list of the top things they do externally to create newness.

b. Now shift the focus to the internal world. Here it is a slightly different story – we try on new beliefs, ideas, dreams, and thoughts without anyone really knowing what is going on in our minds. But what if we want to create newness in how we think about things – do we have the flexibility of the mind to do so or do we have a particular mind-set that we are happy with? Do we say to ourselves, "that's just the way I am" or "it's just my opinion"? Let us look at what it would take to introduce spiritual newness into our lives at this time.

c. Let us start by making a list of the major activities you perform in a day, at home and at work for a full 24 hours.

d. Invite people to take a piece of paper and put a tiny star in the center of the page, with a small circle around the star to represent a 24-hour clock. Write a 0 at North, 6 hours at East, 12 hours at South, and 18 hours at West, and back to 24 hours (or 0). Now ask people to estimate the amount of time they spend on each activity they put in their list. Add colour wedges to show the different activities and how much time is spent on them.

e. Next, invite people to draw a circle about 3 cm out from the clock circle – this represents a year. Ask them to put January at North, March at East, June at South and September at West with December at North again. Ask them to extend their colouring outwards without thinking about it. Just do it.

f. Finally, ask people to draw a third circle and make it an average life span of 84 years – 0 at North, 21 at East, 42 at South, 63 at West and 84 back at North. Again, tell people not to think about it but to extend their coloured wedges outwards to colour in this outer circle.

g. Now let us think about what we have in front of us. Look at the completed circles that represent the way you divide your life.
35 minutes

Reflecting - Ask people to reflect on the following questions in silence, asking each question slowly so they have a chance to think and possibly write their responses.
- What does your life clock suggest to you?
- Are you happy with it?
- What do you want to keep the way it is?
- What would you like to reduce or remove?
- How much time daily would you have to reduce to make a difference in your lifetime?
- What would you like to add?

- How much time would you have to dedicate on a daily basis to make a difference in your lifetime?

Consider the quote:

"If you always do what you have always done, you will always get what you have always got."
15 minutes

Valuing the Experience – Ask: what did you discover about newness tonight? Have the group write their answers on business cards. Have them share with the group.
10 minutes

Embodying the Virtue – Instruct the group to take one positive step to adjust their daily clocks this week to make the difference they would like to see in their annual calendars. End the session with a song.
10 minutes

Resources and References - Paper and pens for writing, coloured pencils or crayons for coloring.

OPTIMISM

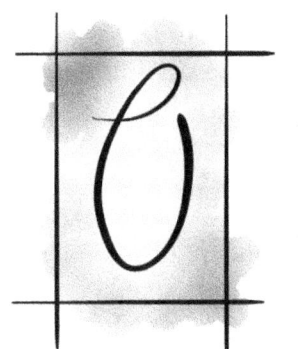

Setting Intention - To bring the virtue of optimism into my worldview.

Meditation - With a commentary of your choice.
20-30 minutes

Experiencing the Virtue – Welcome the group. Let them know that this evening will be about exploring the virtue of optimism. Ask people to share their thoughts on what optimism means to them.

a. Once the group has shared, pass around pieces of paper and a piece of card stock paper (has to be hard enough to lay flat on the knees with beads on it. Alternatively, use clipboards).

b. Ask everyone to draw a big circle in the middle of page. Then pass around a basket or bowl full or beads and ask each person to take a small handful of 20 or so beads.

c. Next ask everyone to take a few moments in silence with the beads and arrange them to create a pleasing view (whatever that looks like to them). Take a few moments and have them just enjoy some silent time creating something that they find pleasing to look at.

d. When everyone is done, ask: what makes your creation pleasing to view? Have them write down 4-6 words outside the circle that describe the qualities they find pleasing in what they have created.

e. Now hear some of the words to describe what makes it pleasing.

f. Now ask: what did it take for you to create this pleasing view? Have them remember their decision-making process, approach, state of mind, and the thoughts and intentions they were having while creating it. With all this in mind, ask them what they had to do/think in order to make this pleasing to view? Consider for a moment, and then hear peoples' answers.

g. Explore the connection between the bead activity and the virtue of optimism. Have the group imagine that the circles on their papers and beads represent a kaleidoscope. Ask the group if they know how kaleidoscopes work, and hear their answers. Explain that kaleidoscopes are full of little beads or pieces of glass, and as you turn them they get shuffled and reconfigured to create a different view. But what is so nice about a kaleidoscope is that each view is pleasing to look at. In a sense, this is what optimism is: *a positive energy that organizes what I see (the optic) into a pleasing view.*

h. Share these dictionary definitions of optimism:

"A disposition or tendency to look on the more favorable side of events or conditions and to expect the most favorable outcome."
"The belief that goodness pervades reality. "
"The belief that good ultimately predominates over evil in the world."
"A tendency to take a hopeful view of things."

i. So now have the group imagine that all the beads are parts of their lives. Optimism is the energy that arranges these bits of your life into a pleasing view.

j. Now have the group take a moment and consider, based on the experience with the beads, how do you, or could you, use the energy of optimism to make decisions about how you organize the bits of *your* life into a pleasing view? Consider this in silence. Hear responses from some (or not - depending on the vibe it might be better to sit quietly).
25 minutes

OPTIONAL ACTIVITIES

(The next step in the activity, to be included depending on the amount of time available)

k. Ask people to get into groups of three or four. Each group will take what they know about this virtue of optimism to create a quiz for the whole group (think of the kind of quiz you see in magazines to measure an aspect of your life). Hand out the quiz template – one per person.

l. As a small group, based on your reflections from this exercise, identify ONE indicator of optimism practically expressed in someone's life. For example: *I find the positive side of negative or difficult situations.* Give them five minutes as a group to create one indicator. Then ask each group to read their indicator out loud.

m. As they read the indicators, ask everyone in the larger group to assess themselves with a score from 1-10 according to how much this indicator is true for them. After each group has offered their question/indicator, ask people to total their scores.

n. Finally, ask for a show of hands: who had 80 and above? 70 and above? etc. See how optimistic people consider themselves to be.
20 minutes

Reflecting – Ask: what was that experience like for you - from the beginning with the beads all the way to the quiz? What was most significant? What did you learn?
10 minutes

Valuing the Experience – Ask: how would you summarize your understanding of the virtue of optimism? Have them write their answers on a business card and share in the group.
10 minutes

Embodying the Virtue - This week we suggest you begin each day with an optimism indicator as part of your morning meditation. Feel it with you throughout the day. End the evening with silence or a song.
5 minutes

Resources and References - Bowl of beads or small bits of colored glass or other pretty colored items, pieces of paper, cardstock for each person, quiz hand out for each person, pens, and stiff paper.

Checking Optimism Quiz

What would be an indicator of my level of optimism today? In your small group, please create ONE indicator for the quiz.

Indicator of Optimism: How optimism would be expressed in a practical way in my day, in my mind, in my life.	On scale of 1-10 (10 being the highest), rate your current level of optimism according to the indicator.
Example: I can find the good in even the most disagreeable people.	

PEACE

Setting Intention - To explore the experience of 'being' peace.

Meditation - With the commentary of your choice.
20-30 minutes

Experiencing the Virtue – Welcome the group. Let them know that this evening will be focused on the virtue of peace. Share some thoughts with the group on peace from the Brahma Kumaris perspective. For example:

For the Brahma Kumaris, the essence of our being and of this organization is 'Om Shanti', meaning, "I am a peaceful soul". As a being of peace, when I am unpeaceful or peaceless, I am experiencing a separation from peace and the core of who I am. Thich Nhat Hanh once said:

"When we can be peace we drop feelings of us versus them and live from a place that sees no separation from others. We make peace with everyone including ourselves."

In this session, invite the souls to participant in three experiments with peace:

1. **Standing Meditation** (2 minutes)
   Ask everyone to stand up, and consider what they stand for. Once you have an idea, stand on it as a foundation for the secure, stable, and peaceful you to emerge. Hold the experience and remember this feeling.

2. **Walking Meditation** (5 minutes)

   Ask people to consider a place they can go that helps them remember their peace. In other words, where you can experience the most peaceful you? Have them walk with this image in their hearts. Walk around the room imagining this place until they hear the bell to come back.

3. **Sitting Meditation** (5 minutes)
   Ask people to consider what they know helps them face all sorts of challenges when they have peace in their heart. Take a moment to consider the wisdom, knowledge, realizations, or experiences they have acquired in life that help them face situations with peace. Sit contemplating this for the next few minutes and absorb the experience of peace.
   20 minutes

Reflecting – Ask: what have you remembered about 'being peace' from all three of the experiments? What do you realize about you as being peace? What are the things that you can think, say, or do that bring you back to your peaceful self? Ask people to take a moment to write their reflections and insights on a note pad.
10 minutes

Valuing the Experience - Ask each person to write a blessings of peace based on what they now understand about peace. The blessing should start with: "May you be peace by..." Place the blessings in a bowl. Have each person choose one and read it out loud.
15 minutes

Embodying the Virtue - This week we suggest that you begin each day with your peace blessing and your reflections on peace. Take them into your morning meditation and absorb and be them throughout the day. End the evening with a song.
10 minutes

Resources and References - *Release Into Peace* by Carmen Warrington on the *Today I Will* CD, paper and pens for writing, small cards for blessings and a bowl to pass them in.

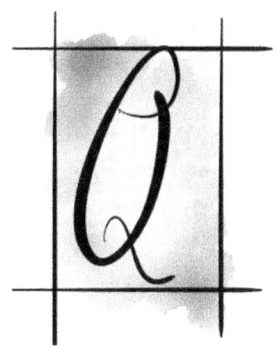

QUICK

Setting Intention - To explore and experience 'quick' as a spiritual virtue.

Meditation - Include a commentary of your choice.
20-30 minutes

Experiencing the Virtue – Welcome the group to tonight's session. Ask them what they think the virtue will be - Q is a hard letter! Let them know that tonight will be about the virtue of 'quick'. Quick is a funny virtue, especially because the reason we come to meditate is often because we are too quick in life – we want to slow down. To be quick is often seen as a sign of racing after your thoughts. Moving too fast means your mind is moving too fast in waste thoughts. So, ask: how can quick be a virtue? Hear responses from the group.

a. Once people have had a chance to share their thoughts, explain that when understood as a spiritual virtue quick is something we want in certain situations. Consider for a moment how it would be to be:
   - Quick to change my attitude
   - Quick to forgive
   - Quick to give something
   - Quick on my feet

b. Now we will play a game of Simon Says. Let us use the game to see how quick we can be. First, ask everyone to put their hand on their nose. Then ask them to put their hand on their chin (but rather than putting your hand on your chin, you, the facilitator, puts your hand on your cheek and wait until people catch on that what you said and did were different).

c. Ask: what does it take to be quick spiritually? Hear their responses. Let the group know that in raja yoga, being quick involves obedience, faith, flexibility, agility, and a nimble intellect! Raja yoga is the practice of a nimble intellect.

d. Explain another game called Hot Potato, first asking if anyone knows the game. Ask everyone to sit in a circle. The purpose of this game is to train ourselves to be really quick about the things we want to be quick about. Explain that instead of a hot potato, we will pass around a treasure box. When the music stops someone opens the box and selects one of the pieces of paper in the box. They will read aloud the instructions written there. We will all be silent for a minute and adopt the suggested spiritual posture as quickly as we can (see statements below to be printed or copied and cut as individual slips and folded and put in box).
40 minutes

Reflecting – Take a few moments to reflect on the experience. Ask the group: what was that experience like for you? What did you learn from it? What did you discover about the practice of being quick (i.e. having a nimble intellect)? What helped you to be quick? What made it easy/hard? What does being quick help us experience, and what is valuable about this? Have the group share their experiences.
10 minutes

Valuing the Experience – Ask: how would you describe the experience of quick as a virtue? Have everyone write their answer on a business card and share what they wrote in the large group.
5 minutes

Embodying the Virtue - This week we suggest you practice being quick. Be quick at seeing the positive, turning a complaint into an appreciation, and other things.
End the evening with a song.
10 minutes

Resources and References - Music - *Absorb and Emit* on the *Lights of the World* CD, A small box with a lid that opens easily, statements listed below printed and cut into strips.

Quick... Become aware you are a soul and not a body!

Quick... Think of someone you love and let them fly free of any expectation you have of them!

Quick... Imagine yourself to be an angel radiating the light of spiritual love!

Quick... Think of someone you should forgive – and forgive him or her!

Quick...Remember a moment today that you feel good about and name the virtues you were experiencing or expressing!

Quick...Experience love!

Quick...Establish a state of inner peace!

Quick...Send love and light to a part of the world in need!

Quick...Change a complaint into an appreciation!

RESPONSIBILITY

Setting Intention - To explore the virtue of responsibility and to feel lighter about the things I am responsible for.

Meditation – Include a commentary of your choice.
20-30 minutes

Experiencing the Virtue – Welcome the group to the evening. Let them know that this session will be about exploring responsibility. We will begin with an activity:

a. Ask each person to reach into their purse, pocket, bag or wallet to find something that has some importance or value to them. For example, it could be a cell phone, watch, a picture, glasses, anything. Ask them to please hand this valuable object to the person sitting next to them on their left. Ask everyone to take care of their neighbour's valuable item for the rest of this session.

b. Ask people to make a mental note of the thoughts/feelings they are having as they realize they have given this object away to someone to take care of - and have received something to care for in return.

c. Remind the group that this session focuses on the virtue of responsibility. Ask them what their understanding of this virtue is? Listen to the responses.

d. Read the Living Values Education Program (LVEP) points from the handout at the end of this section. As a facilitator choose the list of points you feel are most relevant.

e. Ask the group to consider an advanced understanding of this virtue. A lot of people have a lot of things they are responsible for these days, but how is this spiritual? How is 'having a bunch of responsibilities to take care of' a virtue? Hear responses from the group. Once you have heard their answers, suggest that the virtue of responsibility lies in the way we do it. In other words, how we wear our responsibilities.

f. Ask each person to write on a piece of paper a list of the top 3-5 major things, people, or situations that they are responsible for at this time in their life.

g. Once this is done, ask them to consider their relationship to these things they are responsible for. Ask everyone to draw a continuum on their paper, and write a word on each end to describe the kind of relationship we can have with the things they are responsible for. For example, on one end they might write 'light' or 'carefree'. Then on the other end of the continuum they might write 'bondage', 'burden', 'weight', or 'pressure'. Then in between what words might we use to describe the kind of relationship you might have with those things you are responsible for? Hear suggestions.

h. Now, ask people to place their top five things they are responsible for somewhere along this continuum according to the weight they feel it carries.

i. Show your continuum to the person next to you to compare/contrast. Now consider the following questions:
    • What do you notice from this activity?
    • Which responsibility feels the lightest? Why?
    • Which responsibility feels the heaviest? Why?
    • What was the principle or criteria you used to decide the relative weight of your relationship with the things you are responsible for?

    Ask them to share any insights with the person sitting next to them.

j. Now ask the larger group for their responses. Overall, what seems to determine the lightness or weight of a relationship with responsibilities? Listen to their answers.

k. When they are done, share this spiritual principle: **When I feel responsible for something it begins to own me.** How can we carry the things we are responsible for in such a way that they feel light? And so that we feel light? Because it is spiritual, it will be a consciousness we can hold. "Where attention goes, energy flows, and life grows" – this applies to responsibilities too. So what is the consciousness we can hold to help us feel light with regards to the things we are responsible for? Listen for suggestions from the group. Once they have finished, offer that what is required is the consciousness of a trustee. Ask: what is the definition of trustee? What is consciousness of a trustee? Tell them that the key to a trustee consciousness is the idea that "this is NOT MINE".

l. Now ask people to bring out the object they were given earlier and have been keeping for someone in this room. Ask: what is your relationship to this object? Hear their responses.

m. Suggest that they have been trustees for the past thirty minutes, taking care of something that is not their own. The quality of their relationship with the object was based on this awareness. For example, if they had had the object for 20 years they might have begun to claim it, or feel it was their own as the consciousness of 'mine' creeps in. Now ask them to return the object to the other person. How does that feel?

n. Ask people to imagine a world where no one has the feeling of owning anything; we have it, use it, but we do not have the consciousness of mine. What would it take to change our consciousness to this – to a trustee consciousness?

o. Ask everyone to consider a thought - like a mantra - that they would have to adopt to remind themselves of this trustee consciousness. In other words, transforming the consciousness of 'mine' - I carry this alone, I own it - to a trustee consciousness – or, I hold this in trust. At the first sign

of struggle, burden, pressure, etc., they can recall this mantra. It has to be credible for it to work. For some of us the reminder that this is God's task - God is responsible and I am an instrument through whom it is getting done - allows us to remember that this is not mine. For others it might be the universe, etc. Tell them to choose their own thought – to design their own mantra to help transform their relationship with the things and people they have responsibility for so that they can experience the relationship of being a trustee. So they can feel carefree even with a lot of responsibility.
45 minutes

Optional Activity

p. Ask people to look at their continuum and consider the thing on their list that is the heaviest. Now have them select a rock from the basket to represent this burden.

q. When everyone has a rock, ask him or her to place the rock on his or her head. Ask them to hold it and close their eyes. As they feel the weight of this object on them, imagine that it is the thing, person, or situation they feel responsible for. Feel the weight of it. Ask them to slowly bring to mind the mantra they have designed for themselves, and to change their consciousness, or their relationship to this thing. Ask them to say their mantra slowly to themselves and hopefully they begin to feel the trustee consciousness emerging in relation to this thing. Slowly they can lift the rock off their heads. Ask them to keep holding it above their head - it is still there, but not heavy. Then have them bring the rock in front of them – notice the distance between them and this thing. They are not connected to it directly - there is a space between you and it. The space is the safe distance that they have created through the trustee consciousness.
10 minutes

Reflecting – What was that experience like? Have them describe their feelings, insights, and observations. Hear about their experiences.
10 minutes

Valuing the Experience - What is one thing you have learned about the virtue of responsibility through this session? Have them write their answers on business cards. Go around the circle to hear each person read their card.
10 minutes

Embodying the Virtue - This week we suggest that you take one heavy responsibility and transform it through how you think about it. This is to practice the consciousness of being a trustee, an instrument carrying out this task for God. End the evening with a song.
10 minutes

Resources and References - Piece of paper, pens for each, list of responsibility points from the Living Values Education Program, big basket of heavy rocks.

Hand out From Living Values Education Program

Responsibility

3-7 yr. book

- ➤ Responsibility is doing my job.
- ➤ Responsibility is caring.
- ➤ Responsibility is trying my best.
- ➤ Responsibility is doing my share of the work.
- ➤ Responsibility is taking care of things.
- ➤ Responsibility is helping others when they need help.
- ➤ Responsibility is being fair.
- ➤ Responsibility is helping to make a better world.

8-14 yr. book

- ➤ If we want peace, we have the responsibility to be peaceful.
- ➤ If we want a clean world, we have the responsibility to care for nature.
- ➤ Responsibility is doing your share.
- ➤ Responsibility is accepting what is required and carrying out the task to the best of your ability.
- ➤ Responsibility is carrying out duties with integrity.
- ➤ When one is responsible, there is the contentment of having made a contribution.
- ➤ As a responsible person, I have something worthwhile to offer – and so do others.
- ➤ A responsible person knows how to be fair, seeing that each gets a share.
- ➤ With rights there are responsibilities.
- ➤ Responsibility is not only something that obliges us, but also something that allows us to achieve what we wish.
- ➤ Each person can perceive her or his own world and look for the balance of rights and responsibilities.
- ➤ Global responsibility requires respect for all human beings.
- ➤ Responsibility is using our resources to generate a positive change.

SWEETNESS

Setting Intention - To feel, taste, touch, see, and smell the virtue of sweetness.

Meditation – Include a commentary of your choice.
20-30 minutes

Experiencing the Virtue – Welcome the group to the session. Tell them that this evening will be about exploring sweetness. Ask people what they think sweetness is as a virtue. Ask them what they think of it as compared to bitterness? As compared to fakeness? Saccharine? It is not a word that is used with much respect in our world. In fact, it is usually only used in reference to children. Why is this?

a. Once the group has had a bit of a discussion about their initial impressions of sweetness, read the following quote by Anthea Church from the 'Inner Beauty Book of Virtues':

"Sweetness looks for the good in things, for at its heart is the conviction that good is somewhere there in everything, if only you have the patience to discover it. False sweetness is saying that something is good when you haven't taken time to really find out what it is and so have lazily hit on something obvious to comment on. Real sweetness feeds only on reality."

"A bitter tongue makes life bitter; a sweet tongue makes life better. Bitterness is a result of disappointment and pain. To express bitterness is to reveal my own inner hurt. When I realize that my words have become bitter I can bring sweetness into my mind. All I need to do is to remember a pure intention, the innocence of a happy moment or just to remind myself of how sweet I truly am inside. Today let me bring sweetness to life."

b. Tell everyone that we will now experiment with the five senses in order to gather sense organ data about sweetness in order to better understand sweetness as a virtue.

c. Give everyone a hand out (found at the end of this section). We will now experiment with the sensation of sweetness for each of the sense organs and freely association the words that come to mind to describe our experiences.

Taste: Pass everyone a candy or sucker and ask them to taste it. Ask: what surprises you about the taste? What words come to mind when you are tasting the candy? If this taste had a sound, what would it sound like? Have everyone write their answers down.

Sight: Have a stuffed animal or something very sweet to look at. While the group is looking at it, ask: what does sweetness look like? What shape and colour is sweet? Have them write down words in response to the questions.

Touch: Have two different textures available - like silk and flannel or velvet - for people to touch. Ask them to close their eyes and pass the fabrics around for each person to touch in turn. Explore their differences. Ask the group if the textures had a smell, what would they smell like? Have them write down the words they come up with.

Smell: Pass around a fragrant flower and ask everyone to smell it. Ask: what does sweet smell like? If sweetness were a colour, what colour would it be? If sweet had a shape, what shape would it be? Have them write their answers down.

Hearing: Ask everyone to close their eyes and listen to a chime or sweet sound. Ask: how many layers of sweet can you hear? If the sound of sweet had a texture, what would it feel like? Have them write down their answers.
35 minutes

Reflecting – Ask: what was that experience like for you? What experience of sweet was most powerful for you? Why? What did you learn?
10 minutes

Valuing the Experience - Ask souls to summarize the words they would use to describe the experience of sweetness as a virtue. Ask them to include something that would appeal to the senses in their description. Have them write a summary on a business card. Go around circle and hear what everyone has written.
10 minutes

Embodying the Virtue - Suggest that people experiment with being sweet every day this week. End the evening with a song.
10 minutes

Resources and References - 'Inner Beauty Book of Virtues' by Anthea Church, candy to suck on for everyone, cute stuffed animal, pieces of, scented flower, chime/gong, Sweet hand-out (data collection sheet) for each person.

Sweet Handout

Sweet

Sweetness looks for the good in things, for at its heart is the conviction that good is somewhere there in everything, if only you have the patience to discover it. False sweetness is saying that something is good when you haven't taken time to really find out what it is and so have lazily hit on something obvious to comment on. Real sweetness feeds only on reality.

What does Sweetness …

Taste like:

Smell like:

Sound like:

Feel like:

Look like:

TIRELESSNESS

Setting Intention - To bring the virtue of tirelessness into its practical form and see the benefits of it.

Meditation - Include a commentary of your choice.

20-30 minutes

Experiencing the Virtue – Welcome the group to tonight's session. Do not give away what the virtue of the evening is – instead, jump right into the following activities:

a. Without knowing the virtue for the day, ask the group to reflect on their day and identify two experiences from the day that gave them energy. Hear examples from some or have people share their answers with the person next to them.

b. Once people have shared, announce that tonight's virtue is 'tirelessness'. Read the definition of tirelessness from the self-mastery card:

> *"Although the road may be long and hard, as a master my heart is always filled with love for my task. My goal is just a little ways around the next corner, over the next hill. I persevere."*

c. Ask people what they think the definition means, since it sounds exhausting. Hear responses.

d. Share an example of someone who is tireless in the BK family: Dadi Janki, whose body is 100 years old! Yet despite this, she is described as getting younger – what can that mean? Her body is definitely getting older, but her energy is lighter - more joyful, more innocent, more trusting, easy, etc.

e. Ask people to imagine being less tired *after* an activity than beforehand. Ask: have you ever experienced that? Ask people to think of an activity (other than sleep) where they were less tired afterwards than they were beforehand. Share an example (e.g. reading virtue scopes at the fair or doing other service activities).

f. Now walk around the group with a basket with virtue cards in it. Ask people to take a card but not to look at it.

g. After everyone has taken a card, ask people to take a moment to become soul conscious. Then take the basket around the group again, this time selecting a virtue card and passing it to each one while making eye contact with them in order to see the soul.

h. Ask the group: what was that experience like? How was it different than the first time passing the virtue cards around? Hear their responses.

i. Share that the activities we perform are at one level, while the energy we put into the activities is another. When we put spiritual energy into an activity we feel energized and satisfied. In contrast, when we do not use spiritual energy in an activity we often feel drained.

j. Ask people to read the virtue card they have chosen and to consider it and understand it well.

k. Once they have done this, explain that they will now be giving this virtue card to another person. Explain that you will ask them to look at the other person with the energy of soul conscious awareness while you read the virtue card aloud to them (using the word 'you' rather than I to describe the virtue). Now ask them to turn to the person next to them (or some other method for pairing) and do the exercise.

l. Once the exercise is complete, ask them: what was that like? Did you have more energy before or after the activity? Why?

m. With a flipchart draw the addictive cycle or the vicious cycle with a downward spiral. This represents energy being drained at all times, therefore requiring a higher boost of an addictive substance to lift oneself up.

n. Now ask them to describe a virtuous cycle - e.g. to think well of others, to feel good about others, to act well towards others, to feel good about myself, and to receive support/cooperation from others.

o. Have the group begin a discussion based on the observations and insights generated as people looked at the two cycles. During the discussion, suggest that tirelessness is the virtue of generating positive energy through all thoughts, words, and deeds.
35 minutes

Reflecting – Ask: what was that experience like for you? How do you feel at the end of the evening - more or less tired than at the start? Are there any lessons you are taking away with you about how to remain tireless?
10 minutes

Valuing the Experience - Ask everyone to write their summary or definition of tirelessness on a business card, and to read their answers out loud to the group (depending on the size of the group you may not get to hear them all).
10 minutes

Embodying the Virtue - Suggest that people should monitor their energy level this week. When confronted with any task this week, ask them to fill themselves with positive energy and share that energy wordlessly with others as they perform the task. Afterwards, check the effect this method has on their energy levels. End the evening with a song.
10 minutes

Resources and References - *Soul-utions* by Carmen Warrington on the *God* CD, one or more baskets filled with virtue cards (depending on the size of the group).

UNDERSTANDING

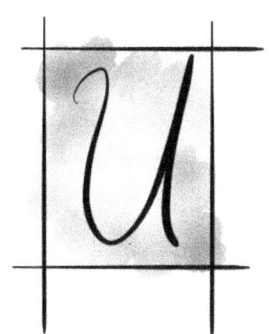

Setting Intention - To experience the virtue of understanding.

Meditation - Include a commentary of your choice.
20-30 minutes

Experiencing the Virtue – Welcome the group to the session. Explain that the virtue of understanding is about getting beneath the surface of situations to see what is really there, or expanding the view of the situation to understand it more completely.

a. Show the YouTube clip of the book 'ZOOM' by Istvan Banyai, or turn pages of real book if people are close enough to see (see below for link to YouTube clip).

b. After seeing ZOOM, ask people for their reactions. How does this book relate to the virtue of understanding? Hear answers from the group.

c. Explain that understanding is often associated with light. For example, people will say that they have 'the light of understanding', or that understanding 'seems to shed light'. 'We are no longer in the dark when we understand', etc. When we feel understood it is like being truly 'seen'. In other words, the light shines on the truth of me or of what I'm trying to express –the meaning of it is lit!

d. Ask people to sit comfortably for a couple of moments and reflect back on their day. Have them remember moments of their day. For example, start by remembering a moment today when you felt good, strong, powerful, and happy – an overall positive experience. Ask: what was the experience? Have people describe the situation to the group. What was nice about it?

e. Next, ask people to write down an experience today that challenged them or left them wondering, 'What happened there?' Have them describe the situation briefly on their piece of paper. Now ask people to look at themselves from a distance through loving, understanding eyes - perhaps the eyes of God - and extend the deepest understanding possible to yourself. Ask: what would you say to yourself to show that you really understood the day's experiences? Have them write the answer down.

f. Now ask people to share their experience of this activity in partners. What does it feel like to be completely understood? What gives the experience of being understood?

g. Once everyone has shared in their pairs, explain that this evening we are all trying to understand what goes on in our world. We are looking at what happens in our lives and each of the different lenses that we use in an attempt to make sense of our world and of our experiences. Some lenses give us the experience of having really 'seen' the truth in a situation. But how do we know when we have seen to the 'truth', given that our vision can be subtly clouded in so many ways? Ask people for a moment to consider the most common lens they use to see and experience the world. Does it have a name?

h. Next, show people a light bulb that has small strips of fabric tied around it and completely covering it. Use one strip of fabric for every lens on the handout at the end of this section. Now screw this bulb into a small lamp and turn the lamp on to see what degree of light shines through. Tell people we will now experiment with some common lenses used to assist us to understand what is happening in our world.

i. Ask people to make a circle. Place printed and cut out pieces of paper describing different lenses on the floor in the center of the circle. Explain that each piece of fabric has a common lens people use to arrive at a certain understanding.

j. Ask six people from the group to each select one piece of paper from the center of the circle. Go around the circle and ask them to read what is written on the pieces of paper out loud. One at a time, after they have read the paper, ask the group to consider each lens from the perspective of these two questions:

- What is the benefit this lens could bring us in helping us to see the light, or to understand a situation for what it really is?
- What could be the limitation of this lens in helping us understand a situation?

k. After hearing about each lens, ask the group or the six people who are holding the papers to place them down and to line up the lenses according to which seems to help us get closer to understanding. Once they have completed this discuss why they put the papers in the order they did.

l. Finally, pass the light bulb around and ask each person to take one piece of fabric off for each of the lenses. Then plug the bulb in again so we can see the light now, without all of the lenses.
35 minutes

Reflecting – Pose reflection questions to the group for them to consider alone. For example, ask: what was the experience like for you? Which lens can be most helpful when attempting to understand things? What lens might you experiment with more to increase your understanding?
10 minutes

Valuing the Experience - Ask people to write on a business card their summary of this virtue. Hear what they wrote.
10 minutes

Embodying the Virtue - This week we suggest that you seek to gain a deeper understanding by getting a broader perspective of the present situation – like in the book 'ZOOM'. Alternatively, you can consider changing the lens through which you are viewing the situation. End the evening with a song.

10 minutes

Resources and References - Lamp, light bulb, small strip of six different colours of cloth, handout cut into strips. Check online for a copy of the book called 'ZOOM', or use the following

YouTube link:
https://www.youtube.com/watch?v=JMhUujrN4iU

Understanding Handout

The Justice Lens
Who is right and who is wrong in this situation? What is right and what is wrong?

The Suffering Lens (aka the Karma Lens)
I'm settling karma; this suffering is for a reason. What is the karma I am settling here and what is the lesson I must learn?

The Business Lens (aka the Bargain/Compromise Lens)
Life is all a give and take – sometimes you win sometimes you lose. We all have to compromise on what we really want. What must I settle for in this situation?

The Learning Lens
Every situation is teaching me something, what is the lesson here? This situation is making me experienced in something – what?

The Problem Solving Lens
What is the problem here? What needs to be resolved/fixed?

Virtues Lens
What virtues are being expressed in the situation? What virtue is being developed in me? What virtue can I be expressing to transform this situation?

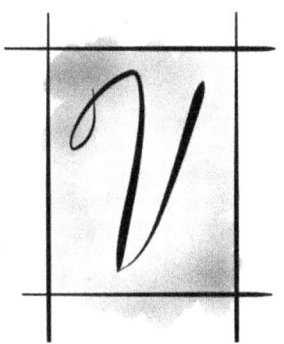

VICTORY

Setting Intention - To know and feel victorious as a collective experience.

Meditation – Include a commentary of your choice.
20-30 minutes

Experiencing the Virtue – Before the session, use masking tape to create a large 6X6 square on the floor.

After the meditation, tell people that you would like to introduce tonight's virtue through a song – *The Sign of a Victory* by R. Kelly

YouTube link: http://www.youtube.com/watch?v=nr5N6Tk_5Is

a. After listening to the song, ask people: what is your understanding of victory? Hear responses from the group.

b. Once everyone who wants to has spoken, suggest that the virtue of victory rests on the premise that something must be conquered. Ask people: what is the 'something' that needs to be conquered? Hear their answers, which may include things like obstacles, problems, battles, etc. Suggest that there could not be the experience of victory without a challenge or obstacles. Explain that the word 'conquest' has the same root as the word quest (like when knights of old were sent on quests to prove themselves). The proof of these quests was demonstrated in two ways:
   - They handled themselves well on the quest (this is the biggest proof)
   - They come back having accomplished the task

c. Now suggest that in the case of the knights, the personal expression of character is equal to the victorious outcome. Consider that in spiritual terms: the expression of character IS the means to achieve the outcome. When I change, the world changes. So my change is a victory because it brings about world change. Ask people what they think of this.

d. Once people have responded, share Dadi's quote: *"To achieve spiritual greatness you must express personal excellence in challenging times."* Suggest another premise of the Raja Yoga view of the spiritual journey: that victory is guaranteed. Ask people to consider this for a moment: how can we know that victory is guaranteed? What subtle proof would we have to even consider this? Ask and wait to hear responses.

e. Suggest that because we want victory so badly - no matter how many storms, how much noise and static, and no matter how much disheartenment and even quitting - we come back. Something in us keeps us trying again and again no matter how much we fail in our own eyes. What keeps us doing that? Perhaps it is a feeling that victory is the ultimate destination. We will not stop until it is achieved. Suggest that in spiritual terms, victory is not to battle, but rather to win your highest stage without battling. That is the holy grail of spirituality.

f. Tell people that tonight they are being given a quest to achieve the Holy Grail. Tell them: your mission, should you choose to accept it, is to transform yourself. You will create the quality of character in yourself that will act as a template/model of what the new world will hold. In other words, be the change you wish to see in the world. Tell the group that they will be given a team challenge that represents some of the hurdles/obstacles that need to be crossed in order to arrive at victory.

g. Before embarking on this quest, and even before knowing what the quest will be, ask them to take a moment and do what knights would do before embarking on a quest: prepare their weapons. Ask: what are the weapons you take with you on this or any quest? Listen to the group's answers.

h. Once everyone who wanted to has spoken, suggest that on the spiritual path there are no physical weapons. Suggest that instead, our weapons are the virtues and powers of the soul. We are equipped with the sword of knowledge and the arrow of yoga power. In the practice of devotion goddesses are portrayed with physical bows and arrows. But these are merely symbolic – vices are conquered with the sword of knowledge, since goddesses cannot be violent.

i. Before the group starts their quest, read this blessing from one of our morning classes:

> *"Before you begin any action, invoke the power required according to the action. Order the spiritual powers as a master, because all of these powers are like your arms; your arms cannot do anything without your orders. Order the power of tolerance...to make a task successful and see how success is guaranteed. However, instead of issuing an order, you become afraid and wonder whether you will be able to do it or not. When you have such fear, you are not able to issue an order. Therefore, be a master creator and become fearless to make every power work according to your order."*

j. Ask each person to take a minute to consider - knowing that they are about to embark on a group challenge, and knowing themselves - what are the powers/virtues you will need to take on this quest with you?

k. Now explain the quest, which is a simple team challenge. In order to succeed the whole group must experience victory. Explain the rules for the Maze Challenge, the instructions for which can be found on the next page. Do the maze.

l. Once the maze is complete, return to the first room. Play the Victory song again but hand out lyrics so that people can sing along. As they achieve victory in the maze, they will feel victorious and the singing will rock!
45 minutes

Reflecting – Ask: what was that experience like for you? Ask people to take a moment to reflect on it. Ask them how they feel. Then ask them to check the two proofs of a victorious quest: did they reach the other side (i.e. achieve their outcome)? Did they use their powers/virtues to conduct themselves in the highest character during the activity?
10 minutes

Valuing the Experience - Ask people to summarize their understanding of victory as a virtue on a business card and to share their answers with the group.
10 minutes

Embodying the Virtue - This week, attempt to see victory in every action you perform each day. End the evening with a song.
10 minutes

Resources and References - Computer/projector, YouTube clip for the song 'Sign of a Victory' (YouTube link: http://www.youtube.com/watch?v=nr5N6Tk_5Is), music and lyrics handout by Ron Kelly, maze page, masking tape to make maze on the floor, bell or glass with pens to make ringing sound.

Quotes for the virtue of victory
- To appreciate the journey, to learn from my mistakes and to rejoice in the knowing - victory is guaranteed.
- Knowing that the outcome will be for my ultimate growth, I joyfully keep my eye on the prize: victory
- Victory is the courage, determination, and ability to evoke the power and support available and to laugh with myself.
- Victory is knowing that although I am a late bloomer, I will bloom.
- Victory is the fearlessness to love with gentleness, respect, giving and caring in order to let go of doubt, knowing positively that you will always succeed.

Sign Of a Victory Lyrics by R. Kelly

I can see the colors of the rainbow,
and I can feel the sun on my face,
I see the light at the end of the tunnel,
and I can feel heaven in its place,
and that's the sign of a victory (x2)

I can feel the spirit of the nations
and I can feel my wings ridin' the winds, yeah
I see the finish line just up ahead now
and I can feel it risin' deep within
and that's the sign of a victory (x2)

Now I can see the distance of the journey,
high and front with all your might,
you open your eyes to global warming,
been through it all, you sacrificed your life
and that's the sign of a victory (x2)

If we believe, we can achieve anything including the
impossible
This I know so let's lift up our heads and raise the flag
yeah yeah
And scream like you want to win now let the games begin!
That's the sign of a victory (x4)
when you keep on fightin', after you lost your strength
that's the sign of a victory

when darkness is all around you, you still find your way
that's the sign of a victory
come on and sing, lift up your voice and sing, stand up, oh
yeah, stand up
sign of a victory ooooohh oh ohhhh

The Maze: Instructions

Draw a grid on the floor using masking tape or masking tape on a plastic tarp. Lay it down on the carpet (see sample below).

				X	
				X	
					X
	X	X	x	X	
	X				
X					

Draw a replica of the maze on a piece of paper and mark a path across it that is only visible to you (the facilitator). There is only one path across the maze, so the job of the team is to find the accurate path across the maze in 15 minutes and get every member of your team across. This will be a process of trial and error. Every error made by someone on the maze will help your team eliminate squares and ultimately find the accurate path across. You will have 10 minutes planning time before stepping onto the maze. In this time you will need to plan your communication strategy because once you step on the maze, the next 15 minutes must be conducted in silence.

Rules for The Maze:
- The team's job is to find their way across the maze and get everyone across in 15 minutes.
- Each time a person steps on the wrong square the facilitator will ring a bell or tap something to indicate a wrong step and the person must make their way back over the same steps to get off the maze (emphasize that each time they do not follow the accurate path back others will be confused).

- Only one person can be on the maze at any given time.
- The path will only ever go forward, diagonally or sideways, never backwards or jumping over squares.
- There must be complete silence while on the maze, so you will need to develop a communication strategy in your planning time.
- No jumping on or off the maze from the side!

Good Luck!

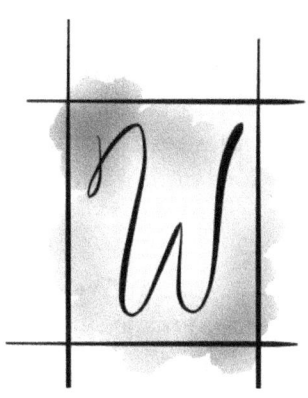

WISDOM

Intention - To explore the spiritual aspects of wisdom from our experiences of both teaching and learning.

Meditation - Include a commentary of your choice.
20-30 minutes

Experiencing the Virtue – Start the session with a check-in on the series. As we are nearing the end of our alphabet series, it is fitting that we explore wisdom. On the self-mastery card wisdom is described as:

> "*As a master I have come to terms with who I am and I recognize my destiny. I flow with it, accepting all. I am no longer deceived by transitory aspects, but live with deeper meaning and purpose.*"

a. To begin, share several personal stories and experiences with teaching and learning from your own life. Teaching and learning is all about knowledge and wisdom. Knowledge is spirit - it is alive. We have a responsibility to use it to transform ourselves and to pass it on to someone else. Knowledge is not mine, I cannot own it but I am a conduit/an instrument for knowledge to pass through.

b. To continue, wisdom is our collective knowing. There is so much to know, especially in Raja Yoga. There is so much to learn about soul consciousness. Just the one thought of "I am a soul" is filled with so much to learn. There are four subjects we take up: knowledge of the cycle, the drama, yoga (i.e. how to be in the point form), and finally the service of sharing with others what we have learned.

c. In preparation for moving into a Wisdom Tree Meditation, tell the group we will experiment with different forms of meditation. These will include walking, standing, lying down and sitting meditations. Each has a different purpose and benefit. Explore that I, the facilitator, will conduct a meditation and ask you to take up one of these positions as you let your spiritual self explore suggestions coming in the commentary.

d. Instruct the group to begin in a lying down position. We will move through the other three positions during our meditation and finish up in the seated position. Have the group stretch out in their lying position, keep their eyes open as you begin your meditation. The lying meditation pose is about healing and forgiveness. Have them breathe deeply. Say:

"Imagine a tall tree in front of you with many wide strong branches extending from its trunk reaching up towards the sky. Imagine yourself lying safely on the first branch of the tree with a member of your birth family. This is about love and innocence."

e. Have the group ask themselves:
    - Who is the other person with you?
    - Who is the teacher? Who is the learner?
    - What happens between the two that takes you beyond what is already known?

f. Now have the group stand up in full meditative awareness for a standing meditation where we connect with the full power of the self. Say:

"Imagine yourself moving up to the next large branch of the tree, where you stand with a member of your extended family of friends and colleagues with love and honesty."

g. Have the group ask themselves:
    - Who is the other person?
    - Who is the teacher? Who is the learner?
    - What happens between the two that takes you beyond what is already known?

h. Now have the group move into a walking meditation about innovation and creativity. As they walk, say:

> *"Imagine you are moving up to a higher strong branch of this mighty Tree of Wisdom. You find yourself walking with an historical figure with love and truth."*

i. Have the group ask themselves:
    - Who is the figure?
    - Who is the teacher? Who is the learner?
    - What happens between the two that takes you beyond what is already known?

j. Now instruct the group to come back and sit down in full meditative awareness in this waiting and listening pose. Say:

> *"Imagine you are on one of the highest branches of the strong and sturdy Wisdom Tree. Sitting with you is your spiritual guide."*

k. Ask yourself:
    - Who is your guide?
    - Who is the teacher? Who is the learner?
    - What happens between the two that takes you beyond what is already known?

l. Gently instruct the group to bring all these images of the Tree of Wisdom back with them into this room.

m. Give the group time and instructions to complete a Writing Exercise. Tell them to take a sheet of paper and record their thoughts about the following questions:
    - What was the wisdom beyond what was already known when I was the learner?
    - What was the wisdom beyond what was already known that came when I was the teacher?
    - Who is my highest spiritual guide and what wisdom am I receiving from that source?

30 minutes

Reflecting on the Experience – Lead the group through a reflective series of questions. Ask:
- What was your experience during the four forms?
- What was your experience of the teacher-learner roles?
- What was significant for you?
- What does that suggest to you about wisdom?

10 minutes

Valuing the Experience – Ask: what insights are you having about wisdom? Have everyone write an insight on their business card. Share these in the large group. Read again the description of wisdom on the self-mastery cards:

> *"As a master I have come to terms with who I am and recognize my destiny. I flow with it, accepting all; I am no longer deceived by transitory aspects, but live with deeper meaning and purpose."*

10 minutes

Embodying the Virtue – Given all that the group has experienced in their meditation on the Tree of Wisdom, the homework this week is to choose one insight that you would like to share with another person this week. Decide who and what and make time to share this living wisdom. End the evening with silence or a song.

10 minutes

'(E)XPANDING' YOUR ZEAL

Setting Intention - To bring a conclusion to the series by celebrating and expanding your zeal!

Meditation - Include a commentary of your choice.
20 - 30 minutes

Experiencing the Virtue – Remind the group that the purpose of this series was to increase our spiritual literacy and to tap into the internal experience of the energy of a virtue. Ask the group why we would have done this. Once you have heard their answers, explain that the reason was to 'eXpand Your Zeal!' Tell the group that this session we will bring a conclusion to the virtues series by expanding your zeal.

a. To begin, share with the group some definitions of zeal from the dictionary:

> *"Fervor for a person, cause, or object; eager desire or endeavor; enthusiastic diligence; ardor."*
> *"Being more concentrated, accurate, etc."*
> *"Fervent or enthusiastic devotion, often extreme or fanatical in nature, as to a religious movement, political cause, ideal, or aspiration."*

b. Next, place all the letters of the alphabet on the floor in the middle of the circle and ask people to consider which two virtues from the series really mattered most to them over the past 25 weeks. Ask each one to select and hold these two letters, possibly the ones they most remember. Ask them to tell the rest of the group about what they attained/experienced about this virtue (this is a nice review of the series also for those who were not there for all sessions).

c. Once everyone has shared, ask: so what is the purpose of having virtue in our lives? Listen to the responses. If you have not already, offer the idea that virtues help to add lift to our wings. They help us fly, bringing quality and enjoyment to life.

d. Continue the session by moving into a personal reflection time. Ask the group to consider in their minds: what is the aim you have for yourself at this time spiritually? Have them write their answers down on the postcard.

e. Getting in touch with our target – focus, concentration, accuracy – supporting yourself in your efforts
   • What are the things I'm doing towards that?
   • What do I know keeps me flying/supports my wings to keep them high?
   • What needs to be strengthened to keep me flying?

f. Now read the following story to the group:

The Story of Deadelus

"After the inventor Daedalus built the Labyrinth, King Minos did not want him to be able to tell its secrets to anybody else, and so he kept Daedalus a prisoner in a tall tower. Daedalus was all alone with only his young son Icarus. Daedalus and Icarus did not like being prisoners, and so Daedalus began to think about how they could get away. He watched the birds flying and he thought how free they were. Watching them, he decided to make wings for himself and Icarus."

"So Daedalus and Icarus began crafting two sets of wings. They made the wings out of bird feathers and wax. Daedalus warned his son to be careful when he was flying: if he went too close to the sea, he might fall in, but if he flew too high in the sky, the heat of the sun would melt the wax on his wings and he would fall. Icarus promised to be careful. So once the wings were finished, they set off for freedom."

"At first everything went well, but after a little while young Icarus got tired of just flying in a straight line. He began to try to do tricks and go up and down. His father told him to behave himself, but Icarus was having too much fun to listen. Icarus kept on going up and up, higher and higher. Suddenly, he realized his wings really were beginning to melt from the heat of the sun. He tried to go back down again, but it was too late. His wings came apart, and he fell down, down, down into the ocean, where he drowned."

"Daedalus was horrified that his son had died, and spent a long time searching for his body. When he found it he flew with his son in his arms until he reached safety. There was nothing he could do but bury his son's body sadly."

g. Invite each person to complete the postcard of 'eXpanding Your Zeal'. Have them share what they wrote with the bigger group in a circle.

h. Now create a standing circle and invite each person to take a turn standing in the center of the circle. Have them tell the group the virtues they have chosen to focus on from earlier in the session. Then in silence, have the person in the centre of the circle turn and give Drishti to each one in the group, and allowing their chosen virtues to shine through. For those who do not know, Drishti is looking at the third eye in the center of the forehead and seeing the soul as God sees them, full of all virtues. Everyone in the circle should offer soulful, heart-felt support to that soul through Drishti, looking at the person seeing him or her with the chosen virtues. This can be a very powerful experience for those who have been together throughout the entire virtues series.
50 minutes

Reflecting – Ask everyone to think about all the steps in the experience tonight. Ask: what stood out for you, and why was that important to eXpanding your zeal? What did the steps this evening suggest about eXpanding Your Zeal? Have them share their answers with a partner and then share the highlights in the group.
15 minutes

Valuing the Experience – Ask: what do you now understand about 'eXpanding' Your Zeal? Have them write their answers on business cards and share them with the group.
10 minutes

Embodying the Virtue – As you leave this last session on the virtues, consider a method for yourself to keep the virtues alive on a daily basis at home, at work and in your community. Plan to keep a journal of your practice. End the evening with a closing song.
10 minutes

Resources and References – post card handout for eXpanding your Zeal.

eXpanding Your Zeal

What do I know keeps me flying and supports
my wings to keep them high?

What needs to be strengthened to keep me flying?

*"You fly with wings of zeal and enthusiasm. This zeal is the greatest
power for you, to make life not dry and tasteless.*

*Experience the sweetness of zeal and enthusiasm to maintain the flying
stage."*

End Note

And that's it ... our exploration of 26 virtues over as many weeks! As we said in the opening pages - we are inspired by the Brahma Kumaris World Spiritual Organization (www.brahmakumaris.org) to help build a values-based world. We loved designing these sessions that gave people both an opportunity to experience the energy of a wide array of virtues and to build a larger spiritual vocabulary.

We had pure fun setting our intention, designing a group activity, facilitating it, not knowing what would happen or whether the energy of the group would culminate in naming the virtue. And it was always a learning opportunity for all of us. Reflection on what happened provided real gems that allowed the virtues to shine through.

So what can you do when things just don't seem right? When you wish all the people around you would just be nicer to each other, to help make the world a better place to live in. So who's going to start – them or you?

You – of course! Changing the world starts with each one of us. This guide shares lots of creative ways for expressing the innate goodness of the soul (especially in challenging times) in group settings.

Are you ready for a 26-week commitment? Do it - its great fun! In this guide you will find 25 plans for a series of one-hour sessions that take you through the alphabet from A to Z to explore virtues like accuracy, benevolence, cooperation, and many more until you get to zeal!

Let us know how it went at Halifax@ca.brahmakumaris.org. We hope you enjoy the experience as much as we did. Modify and create your own virtues series to encompass so many other virtues not included here. We'd love to hear from you.

Have fun! Dive in! And explore the inner world of virtues.
Wishing you all the best,
Debbie and Judy

www.ingramcontent.com/pod-product-compliance
Lightning Source LLC
Chambersburg PA
CBHW070927290526
45795CB00001B/455